Introduction

1 Early days in schoo
Lack of independence
Less developed lingui
Made to read and wr
   emotionally read

Introduction

Underachieving boys? Historically, to a certain degree, it has always been thus. With more girls passing the eleven-plus than boys, moves had to be made to ensure that equal numbers of girls and boys attended grammar schools. So the bar was raised for girls. In the 1970s, concerns that girls were faring less well than boys in maths and science prompted moves to address the issue. These proved largely successful. Many would argue that a move to more coursework than examinations, while not happening for precisely that purpose, ensured that girls would always retain the upper hand across the board. The fact is that the issue of boys' underachievement is not going away. We are now armed with a plethora of assessment details and statistics that spell it out loud and clear. Boys continue to be outperformed at the Foundation Stage and have been since assessment at that phase began. Similarly, in all subjects at Key Stage 1, since these tests began, the pattern has been that girls have outperformed boys. At Key Stage 2, boys are only coming out slightly on top in maths, and a huge gap has begun to appear by this time in English, most notably in writing. Indeed boys' writing is something that is engaging everyone's attention, from primary schools right through to Year 11. At Key Stage 3, girls have the upper hand in all three subjects, again most notably in English, and again it is a pattern that is not going away. By the time we get to GCSE, girls are now outperforming boys in every subject, with again the largest gaps in language-based subjects but with equivalent gaps developing in subjects such as design technology – for similar reasons, a far greater emphasis than ever before is on the written element.

The gender gap of about 10 per cent at five A*–C has been with us since GCSEs were introduced. At A level, it used to be the case in the early 1970s that boys finally caught up and outperformed girls. Not any more. In recent years, the situation has reversed. Last year 58 per cent of entries to university were young women and there are now more young women in management training colleges. While there has been a general increase in educational standards year upon year, the truth is – and this is the most accurate way to describe the situation – boys have singularly failed to catch up!

There is no simple, single reason why boys underachieve. At the same time, neither is there a quick fix, not least of all because no two boys are alike. Neither, for that matter, are any two groups of boys alike, although there can be a fair amount of common ground. Over recent years, there has been a debate that has tended to focus on the reason as being either the 'laddish culture' or inappropriate teaching and learning styles. Yes! I say, both of those – plus at least 20-odd more.

The fact that the issue is so complex does not, of course, prevent people from often applying what I would consider to be a knee-jerk reaction that can often change what is going on in schools in a negative way, often not only to the detriment of boys but also to the detriment of girls. Single-sex grouping in a comprehensive situation and seating students boy/girl/boy/girl both spring to mind and both receive some attention in *Breaking through Barriers to Boys' Achievement* (Wilson, 2006) and here.

The main work contains a training tool, similar to the checklist that can be found on pages 92–95, that will enable you to focus very specifically on the barriers that impact on the boys in your school, Key Stage, year group or class. Clearly no two cohorts or even groups of boys are the same, and therefore often a distinctly different set of barriers affect different groups. Subsequently, I believe that by using this method it is possible to focus more accurately on your boys' needs. I believe that a whole-school approach that begins with researching into the precise nature of the problem in this way needs to be followed by raising the awareness of the issues across the whole school. I believe that in developing a project to help raise boys' achievement it is vital that the whole-school community actively engages with the issues and understands that whatever is to be done to address the attitude, behaviour and, subsequently, the performance of boys will also have massive, positive effects on the girls. Anyone in any doubt might be asked to consider who it is in their class who provides the greatest challenges and takes up most of their time. The development of strategies and the subsequent monitoring of their successes, of course, follow the raising awareness stage. Again, it is hoped that many of the tried and tested strategies touched upon here may be useful in your context.

Common themes will quickly become apparent, not least those related to boys and literacy. One of the other most significant themes is the desperate need that we have to develop boys' ability to reflect – the weakest card in their hand. Also included here is a very brief look at appropriate teaching and learning styles and an approach to teaching and learning that hits all the right buttons for boys without disadvantaging girls. You are also invited to consider how effective your school's reward system is in motivating boys, and how to develop a positive-achievement culture in school that allows boys to feel that it is indeed a good thing to achieve. Linked very closely to this issue is perhaps one of the most powerful and significant barriers to boys' achievement – peer pressure. Here I touch upon how we need to deal with the menace that I refer to as the 'Peer Police'. I also make many references to the need for constantly engaging boys in a dialogue about the issues. They are, after all, the real experts.

A common theme through many of the strategies is an emphasis on how we might in our work simultaneously focus on what I call a 'caring masculinity' – in the hope that in our work we always have at least as part of our focus, the need to turn out decent young men.

All of the barriers are expanded upon in greater detail, with additional practical approaches, in *Breaking through Barriers to Boys' Achievement*, but I hope that you will find this slim volume either a useful and practical introduction or indeed a useful additional resource.

Good luck!

Gary Wilson

Early days in school

Concept

Barrier I Lack of independence prior to starting school

The ability of many boys to meet coursework deadlines in Year 11 originates way back in their educational experience. Many Reception and Nursery teachers tell stories of boys, standing helplessly in the cloakroom at the end of the day, arms stretched out by their sides waiting to have their coats put on. They tell of many boys frequently sitting on the benches in the cloakrooms after PE while girls get them dressed, doing up their shirt buttons and fastening their shoelaces. By doing everything for boys, we are clearly hampering their abilities to become independently functioning human beings, let alone independent learners.

One headteacher relates how, when conducting a teaching and learning questionnaire with 9 and 10 year olds, she was amazed at the replies to one question in particular: 'Who is responsible for your learning?' Twenty-eight girls and 40 boys were included in the survey. In response, all 28 girls wrote 'I am' or 'me'. How many of the boys? All? Half? Ten? Less than ten? The answer was none. Not one of them. All of them put their teacher or their headteacher or their parents. On numerous occasions I have shared these findings at parents' evenings, and they laugh! 'Ah well, boys eh! What do you expect?' 'Bless them!' Then I turn on them – 'But it's your fault!' Clearly there is a great need to communicate to parents the relationship between developing independence, and becoming an independent and effective learner – at any age, but preferably by starting when they are very young. Home visits can play a tremendous part – meetings in school can help parents see that there are common issues and often things they can learn from each other.

Application

- Life-sized cut-out boy and girl with speech bubbles can be usefully employed outside Early Years' classrooms.
    - 'I can fasten my own laces – Ben'
    - 'I remember my bag for school without being reminded – Sam'
    - 'I can help prepare for snack time – Matthew'
- Parents can be encouraged to add speech bubbles themselves from a bank of 'at home' balloons.
    - 'I can keep my room tidy – Ben'
    - 'I help prepare meals at home – Sam'
- Pupils can also be given certificates matching their achievements to display at home.

Independence skills

Start with a limited number of tasks and then slowly increase the number. For example:

- **Do you encourage your son to help around the house?**
  If not, then begin by getting him to sort washing into colours, socks into pairs and so on.
- **Do you encourage him to dress himself?**
  If not, then begin by encouraging him to choose what kind of clothes to wear, discussing the practicalities of what he chooses and so on.
- **Do you encourage your son to help prepare meals?**
  If not, then include setting the table as a joint activity, counting and sorting cutlery and laying the correct number of places.
- **Do you encourage your son to help tidy things away after meals?**
  If not, then include returning items to the correct places in the cupboards or fridge.

Concept

Barrier 2 Less developed linguistically on entry to school

Prior to school, research suggests that girls use between ten and thirty times as much language in their play. At the first point at which pupils are assessed in school, the Foundation Stage Profile, girls have been in front in all 13 categories in which they have been measured over the last three years. Some of the most significant gaps are in literacy, with 41 per cent of boys meeting or working beyond early learning goals in language for communication and thinking, as opposed to 55 per cent of girls – a gap of 14 per cent. With regard to linking sounds and letters, the gap is 10 per cent, in reading the gap is 8 per cent and writing 12 per cent.

I regularly deliver parents' evenings about how parents can help their boys achieve. With regard to literacy, I make my usual points about how, for example, only about half of the homes in this country now possess tables, around which families sit and eat. I point out that in countries such as France and Spain there are significantly less problems with oracy. I also recount my horror at discovering that within one large town in England, membership of the library among under-fives amounted to approximately 75 per cent girls. Now that's not the boys' fault is it? I pose the question: 'Why is that? Are parents saying – he's a boy, he won't be interested in reading? Or, he's a boy, he'll only misbehave and show me up?'

We have to get the messages across to parents about the huge role they have to play in engaging boys in language-based activity if we want to reduce this particular barrier to boys' achievement. What we *do not* want, however, is for parents to increase pressure on boys to be avid readers, perfect spellers, producing a beautiful cursive handwriting. The messages we need to communicate are fairly simple.

Application

Messages for parents pre-school

- Try to ensure that he sees adults reading in the home, particularly older males, and talking excitedly about their reading.
- Where possible both parents should read to him (and do not stop the moment he can read for himself!).
- Play board games together.
- Play imaginatively together with toys, creating characters' voices and encourage him to do the same.
- Find opportunities for discussion related to films or programmes watched together on television.
- Limit leisure time spent passively in front of screens.
- Make meal times social occasions where you discuss everyone's day.

What are the issues around boys and literacy?

- Girls currently start school at a significant advantage in their use of language.
- Girls currently outperform boys in all literacy-based tests including The Foundation Stage Profile, Key Stage 1 Reading and Writing, Key Stage 2 Reading and Writing and Key Stage 3 English.
- The largest gender gaps at GCSE are in language-based subjects.
- Boys who are not encouraged to talk through their ideas have difficulty putting pen to paper.
- Boys who are rarely given the opportunity to verbalize their feelings about something that they have learned through a process of review and reflection cannot become effective learners.
- Boys who are not encouraged to talk and express their feelings often resort to other means.
- These boys often become the kind of men who cannot subsequently express their feelings in adulthood.

A person who had worked as a Samaritan for 14 years recently told me that she had *never* spoken to a young man on the other end of the telephone in all that time.

Barrier 3 Made to read and write before being physically or emotionally ready

There is one country in the developed world where there are no concerns about boys' underachievement. Where? Finland. One of the key differences between their system and ours is that formalized schooling does not begin until the age of seven. There is no evidence to suggest that an early start to formal schooling benefits children. Indeed, I believe that currently we give many boys an early taste of failure that remains with them to at least some degree for the rest of their lives. How? By insisting that they read and write before they are ready and able, either physically or emotionally.

> In short, the early age which we teach reading favours girls, on average, and puts boys at a disadvantage. As a consequence, boys, on average, do not feel as valued as girls in the central learning tasks of elementary school. In therapy with boys, we often hear them describe themselves as losers and failures … and their disheartening struggle as students easily comes to define their lives as boys.
>
> (Kindlon and Thompson, 1999)

With regard to writing, for example, how many boys or, indeed, men do you know who have developed a beautiful, cursive handwriting style of which they have been justifiably proud? On the other hand, how many boys do you know who have spent their entire school career listening to the teacher cooing over a neighbouring girl's work – 'That's lovely and neat dear' – while a grimace has been all that has greeted their efforts. Whenever I talk to five- and six-year-old boys about writing, the comments that I frequently get are not so much about how writing is boring or about how they hate certain types of writing but rather they talk about how they hate it, 'because it hurts'.

Application

Pupil interview (no writing!)

You may like to find out about boys' attitudes to literacy, and even to detect where any negativity (if any) originates from. Try the following questions.

- Do you enjoy writing?
- Have you always?
- Do you have any happy/unhappy memories about writing?
- Are you a good writer? Why? Why not?
- Is handwriting an issue for you?
- Do you prefer a particular type of writing?
- Are there any subjects where you particularly don't like the kind of writing you're asked to do? Why not?
- Do you find it easier to write if you've had a chance to talk through your ideas first, or don't you mind?
- How are you at planning your writing?
- Do you prefer writing a little bit at a time, then coming back to it later?
- How are you at checking through your work afterwards?
- Do you like it when your teacher reads out your work to the rest of the class? Or puts it on display?
- What's the best way of getting you to write?
- What's the best way of turning you off writing?
- Are you a keen reader? Why? Why not?
- What are your earliest memories of reading?
- Happy ones? Any unhappy ones?
- What do you read the most?
- What encourages you to read/what discourages you from reading?
- Do you like class discussion?
- Group discussion?
- Question and answer sessions?
- Listening to the teacher?
- Discussing ideas with a partner?
- Reading out loud in front of the class?
- Classroom drama?

Concept

For decades, one school in New York admitted five-year-old girls and six-year-old boys in order to compensate for the differential in development until it finally bowed to the pressure of some parents to admit their 'school ready' five year olds. Steve Biddulph argues the case for all schools to consider classes where boys are a year older than girls. In Waldorf schools in America, as part of their arts-based curriculum, a 'pictorial' introduction to reading is heavily emphasized rather than a more formalized approach. A Waldorf school head is quoted as saying: 'If you start teaching it any earlier, it looks as if all your boys have reading disabilities.' Many believe that this is a significant root cause of such a disproportionate number of boys being labelled as having learning difficulties.

In many boys, several of the reflexes with which we are born are still not integrated by the age of four and five. Most notably, in the case of writing, cross-lateral reflexes are often still 'switched on'. This reflex is the one where if you turn one arm and shoulder over in your cot, your entire body turns over. A simple test that shows whether or not this is integrated is as follows: Ask your four or five year old to stand still, eyes shut and arms out in front. Gently turn his head. If an arm or both arms follow, then the reflex is not integrated and, you might say, he is not ready to scan a page from left to right. In other words, he is physically not yet in a state of readiness to read or write.

While it is clearly not the solution to the problem, several activities can help not only to integrate cross-lateral reflexes but also to improve pupils' abilities generally in handwriting, creative writing, reading and speaking, and listening.

Application

Activities for writers

With each hand in the air, draw imaginary bubbles of different sizes as they float up.

Trace circles in the air with two hands held together. Follow your hand movements with your eyes only. Keep your head still. Keep your lips and teeth together.

We use a phenomenal number of muscles when we write – some of us even screw up our faces! In fact, you might argue, we use as many as we do in some sports, yet how often do we start to play a sport without warming up? Try the following warm-up activity for writing:

- Take two pieces of scrap paper (A5).
- Place one in each hand and screw them both up (enthusiastically!).
- NOW, without using anything to rest on or the other hand, straighten them both out.

Concept

Barrier 4 Many writing activities seen as irrelevant and unimportant

Question: What is the best way of turning you off writing?
Year 10 boy: Having to copy something out.

I recently came across a science department in a high school where they believe the reason they eradicated a significant gender gap (in favour of girls) was because they banned copying from books and from boards.

> Instead, we provided them with every kind of all-singing, all-dancing revision materials, engaged them in producing mind maps, and changed from a position of practical work being a reward to practical work being an entitlement. It turned the boys around.

Writing with a real sense of purpose and a clear audience will engage boys best. Incorporate ICT skills and with many boys you have already significantly increased their chances of success. Use these key factors to produce cross-phase work and you start to hit even more buttons. The interaction that is necessary for Year 10 boys to create, for example, a story for local nursery-aged children calls into play a whole range of new skills. Discussion, without exception, will significantly improve the quality of boys' writing. Similarly, the production of a series of tips and hints or 'Rough Guide' to the high school, produced by Year 8 boys for Year 6 boys prior to their arrival at their new school, means a significant amount of cross-phase discussion and planning. Subsequently, the quality of outcome will tend to reflect the value placed upon the exercise by all concerned.

A significant proportion of the barriers to many boys' achievement are literacy related. This section provides you with a template to improve boys' writing and strategies for planning, preparing and structuring their work more effectively. Engaging boys with reading and guiding them on their reading journey is also dealt with here.

Application

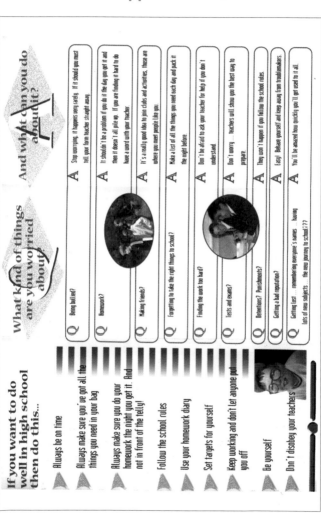

If you want to do well in high school then do this...

- Always be on time
- Always make sure you've got all the things you need in your bag
- Always make sure you do your homework the night you get it. And not in front of the telly!
- Follow the school rules
- Use your homework diary
- Set targets for yourself
- Keep working and don't let anyone put you off
- Be yourself
- Don't disobey your teachers

What kind of things are you worried about?

And what can you do about it?

Q Being bullied?
A Stop worrying, it happens very rarely. If it should you must tell your form teacher straight away

Q Homework?
A It shouldn't be a problem if you do it the day you get it and then it doesn't all pile up. If you are finding it hard to do have a word with your teacher

Q Making friends?
A It's a really good idea to join clubs and activities, those are where you meet people like you.

Q Forgetting to take the right things to school?
A Make a list of all the things you need each day and pack it the night before.

Q Finding the work too hard?
A Don't be afraid to ask your teacher for help if you don't understand

Q Tests and exams?
A Don't worry ... teachers will show you the best way to prepare

Q Detentions? Punishments?
A They won't happen if you follow the school rules

Q Getting a bad reputation?
A Easy! Behave yourself and keep away from troublemakers.

Q Getting lost ... remembering everyone's names ... having lots of new subjects ... the new journey to school???
A You'll be amazed how quickly you'll get used to it all.

Concept

Boys and writing

3. Do they *need* to write it down?

b. Concept maps?

2. Are they allowed time for reflection (inward and outward) first?

a. Bullet points?

1. Is there a clear audience?

4. Is there a better format for writing it down? Can we give them a choice of format?

5. Do they possess the skills to structure their writing?

6. Is it 'chunked' down?

10. How engaging is the writing activity?

7. Is feedback fast and useful and do we show how much we value their work?

9. How clear is the purpose?

8. Do we have a culture in school that enables them to take pride in their writing?

Application

1. Is the 'audience' that pile of dog-eared books on your desk – or is the audience someone *real*? The latter will always produce the best results.

2. Time to think and, above all, time to discuss are vital precursors to boys' writing. Probably the most important element in the whole process.

3. We do too much writing in school! We even use it as a means of control sometimes, and – heaven forbid – some schools *still* use writing as punishment. Less writing, but of better quality, would suit everyone best – particularly boys.

4. Bullet points are acceptable in English Key Stage 3 answers. Then surely they must be acceptable elsewhere? Mind maps and concept maps are fantastically boy friendly – non-linear and without a lot of words.

5. Possibly not – but the last thing boys need is death by writing frame. Producing the same stilted, pre-produced writing frame time after time can kill it stone dead. Produce them live, there and then, in that particular context, for that particular group, for that particular purpose.

6. 'Boy-friendly chunks' work well with five year olds right up to reticent 16 year olds completing coursework.

7. Oral feedback is best – backed up with written feedback of quality. For boys, it is all about the genuine interest of another human being, not marks or grades. Submarine grades, below C level, signal failure to many.

8. In fact, does your school have a culture that enables boys to take pride in anything? Or do the Peer Police put a stop to that?

9. Remember! Boys are the best barometers of good teaching!

10. Copying from a book or the board is the number one switch off for boys and writing. How often can you get away with asking them to imagine they are a leaf in autumn and writing about the experience?

Concept

Barrier 5 **Difficulties with structuring written work**

Before Smart boards, we in teaching were often guilty of 'death by worksheet', flooding students' desks, exercise books, homework planners, bags and bedroom floors with the things. Now we are in danger of creating 'death by writing frame'. All the evidence suggests that constantly presenting boys with the same tired, barren writing frames has limited value. Top of the list of what is most effective is 'live' modelling – as Einstein said 'not just a good way of teaching something – but the only way.' Live modelling is best carried out using the OHP or Smart board, creating a template and exemplary writing there and then for that very specific set of circumstances with that very specific group of students. There are many other supporting mechanisms that can be used – for example, graphic organizers and also the use of mapping can be extremely powerful. Fundamental though of course is that boys are enabled to see and clearly understand the constituent parts of a piece of writing in order that they can emulate it.

At the earliest stages of writing, the model presented by writer and educationalist Pie Corbett exemplifies this very well:

- First, encourage pupils to *imitate* a story structure and thus internalize the pattern of the story.
- Then, encourage them to *innovate*; in other words, to manipulate the pattern of the story.
- Finally, they *invent* their own.

As at any age, this practice needs to be first performed orally. If boys do not have the opportunity to talk through their ideas before they write, many will be incapable of writing.

> **TIP:**
> Learning mats come into their own for many boys, who tend to be systemizers and need to see the constituent parts of something in order to understand more clearly how they work, before they can make it work for them.

Application

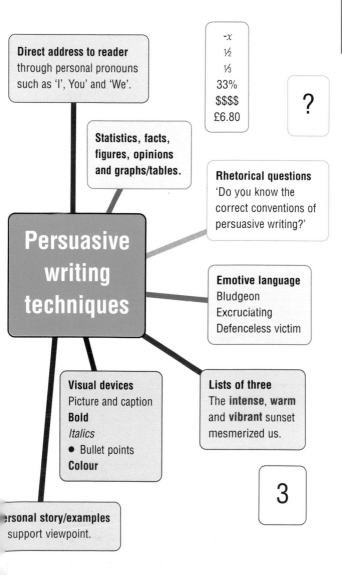

Direct address to reader through personal pronouns such as 'I', You' and 'We'.

$-x$
$\frac{1}{2}$
$\frac{1}{3}$
33%
$$$$
£6.80

?

Statistics, facts, figures, opinions and graphs/tables.

Rhetorical questions 'Do you know the correct conventions of persuasive writing?'

Persuasive writing techniques

Emotive language Bludgeon Excruciating Defenceless victim

Visual devices Picture and caption **Bold** *Italics* • Bullet points **Colour**

Lists of three The **intense**, **warm** and **vibrant** sunset mesmerized us.

3

ersonal story/examples support viewpoint.

Learning mats, containing information such as that above, (typically A3, colourful, illustrated and laminated), provide boys with a very visual and clear set of prompts and guidelines to help them incorporate all the appropriate elements in their writing. Infinitely more effective than a series of barren empty boxes.

Concept

The hint of a challenge can often help focus boys' minds and help them to structure.

A structured approach such as the one devised by educational consultant Ros Wilson, namely 'Big Writing', has proved to have had a significant impact on boys' writing. The process involves creating the right environment for learning, which may involve dimming the lights, producing an appropriate ambience using music and whatever else may feel appropriate.

At the youngest level, the pupils will have been familiarized with, and seen constantly and prominently displayed, the punctuation pyramid, which will provide them with constant prompts – and, in many boys' eyes, challenges with regard to their use of punctuation. (The top level of the pyramid represents level 1 and so on.)

```
              .
            . ?
          . ? , !
        . ? , ... ! ' ' '
      . ? , ... ! ' ' ' : ; ( )
```

The focus is deliberately divided into a series of boy-friendly chunks, at various times in both the writing process and during the teacher and pupil sharing of outcomes. The various elements on which the focus is placed is as follows:

Vocabulary
Connectives
Openings
Punctuation

Again, these elements are displayed at all times and constant reference made to good vocabulary as WOW words. During the writing and the sharing, the focus varies as shown below:

- 10 minutes – check for types of punctuation.
- 20 minutes – check for use of ambitious vocabulary.
- 30 minutes – check for different openers and connectives used.

Application

Boy-friendly chunks

- A template for poetry based on abstract nouns: Anger.
    Anger is bright red, like a chilli on fire,
    It smells burnt, black and smoky,
    It tastes painful and lumpy,
    It sounds fierce, growling like a lion,
    It feels hot like a volcano,
    It lives deep inside your head.
                            Nathan Crossland, 10, Chickenley School
- Can you write a story in ten words?
    The shortest story in the world is by Edgar Allan Poe:
    'For sale, one pair of baby shoes, never worn.'
- Or mini sagas: stories written in 50 words.

The reason of man and the instinct of the beast

A woodsman lived in a cottage with his baby. By day he hewed timber, his trusted Alsatian guarding the infant. One evening, he found turmoil, the cot overturned, the dog with bloodied muzzle. He shot it. A muffled whimper followed from the unharmed child. Nearby lay a dead Siberian wolf.

Jonathan Stoker

Converted

The lion gazed dreamily at its cut paw. What a nice man that missionary, who, on hearing the moans, had fearlessly come over and pulled out the thorn. The lion smiled lazily as it licked the missionary's boots – a little tough, perhaps, but the rest had certainly been very tender.

Jack Union

Concept

Barrier 6 Reticent to spend time on planning and preparation

The mapping of ideas is an extremely powerful tool for boys, enabling them to gather ideas together in a way that lets them save time, focus clearly on an issue and group thoughts in a non-linear fashion. All of these have strong appeal for 'big picture thinkers', that is, most boys. For them, the outcome of the planning process *has* to provide them with a view of exactly where something is going. Without it many will fail to engage or will soon flounder. Mapping gives them that clarity, enabling them to always see the big picture as they work through the process that follows. It also delivers it in a way that is not linear, a real bonus for boys. They are also a very efficient way for many boys to take notes. Day after day learners are encouraged to take notes and, more often than not, the expectation is that the notes will be taken in a linear form. The brain prefers to store information by association, in a pattern, not unlike the pattern created by a mind map The more boys work with this approach, the better it will be for them. What is more, they are more likely to refer to their notes if they are presented in a non-linear form.

Many boys have a particular problem with regard to researching something prior to writing. By the end of high school, it is possible that many boys still think that researching means cutting and pasting something from the internet straight onto a blank word document, sticking their name on the bottom and then just handing it in – without even reading it. That they have reached that point in their school career without having developed those skills is something that we have to address.

Application

One approach to developing boys' research skills using ICT:

1. Provide a list of ten appropriate websites of variable quality.

2. Ask students to select the three most useful/appropriate and, using the highlighter tool, highlight them on the list.

3. Ask them to cut and paste extracts from each website onto a word document.

4. Ask them to select useful sections, using the highlighter tool.

5. Ask them to summarize or précis the information, and use quotes if necessary.

6. Ask them to present evidence of the whole process, together with the final result.

Far from feeling like just 'more work', this approach can supply many boys with a system that many will appreciate – not least because it prevents some of them sensing the fear and helplessness they feel when asked to 'do some research'. For some boys, starting out into the internet can feel like starting out into deep space.

Concept

Barrier 7 Reading fiction perceived as a female province

For many boys, particularly as they pass into the high school, reading can seem to be some kind of secret code known and understood only by teachers and women. They see their mums reading at home and, indeed, for many it was only their mums that read to them before they started school. The fact that teachers and girls seem quite capable of eliciting meaning from literature, and even seem to enjoy it, can often alienate many boys, making them feel inadequate and stupid. The Peer Police, patrolling the boundaries of gender-approved behaviour, do not help either!

We need to demystify the whole process and subsequently engage and enthuse boys in reading fiction. 'Boys *need* to read fiction like I need to breathe oxygen!' is an exhortation I have made many, many times. It is not about the need to increase their vocabulary, improve their spelling or help them with their punctuation, it is about developing what, for many boys, is the weakest area of their learning process – their ability to reflect.

The Harry Potter series was hugely successful in getting boys reading, of that there is little doubt. Many boys, however, uncertain where to go for advice or ideas, read and re-read the same books over and over again. A simple map, such as the one on the opposite page can be used in a library, with covers (downloaded from the internet and shrunk) stuck on the map in appropriate places to reflect your library's book stock.

> **TIP**
> Reading ladders, in the form of posters or bookmarks, can list a range of books in the same genre, with easier titles at the bottom and harder titles recommended as they move up the ladder. The sense of challenge can help engage boys in a more rewarding reading journey.

Application

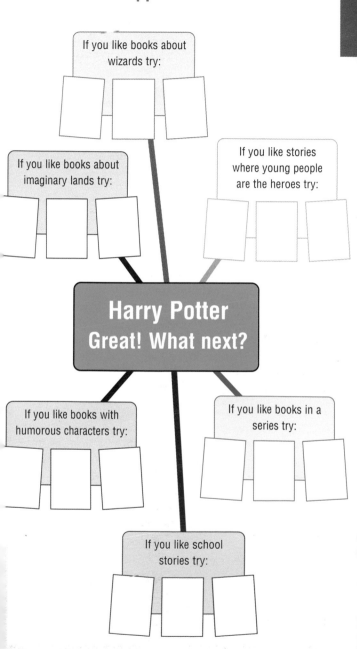

If you like books about wizards try:

If you like stories where young people are the heroes try:

If you like books about imaginary lands try:

Harry Potter Great! What next?

If you like books with humorous characters try:

If you like books in a series try:

If you like school stories try:

Concept

More detailed recommendations on how to get boys reading fiction appear in *Breaking through Barriers to Boys' Achievement*, including:

- creating boy-friendly areas in the library
- introducing literary-based events to engage and inspire
- suspending the timetable at various points in the year to create whole-school reading weeks
- effectively using your own peer leaders to promote reading.

What often comes as a surprise to schools is that, once given the incentive, boys can often get extremely involved in reading fiction. One local primary school I know had a hugely thriving boys' lunchtime bookclub where boys very enthusiastically share their reading experiences. Engaging boys in the high school with Carnegie Medal shadowing (www.carnegiegreenaway.org.uk/shadowingsite) can often inspire deeper interest. Again, the hint of competition giving it that added spice. Better still, one high school I know engaged some of its boys (and girls!) in Greenaway medal shadowing (the primary equivalent), working in consultation with pupils in their feeder primaries.

Our Year 8s choose books they want to read to the Year 3 class. We spend the morning with them, reading and discussing the books. They even spend playtime together. On our second visit to the primary school, our children post a book review onto the official Greenaway shadowing site and then they help the Year 3 pupils do the same. The third meeting is a drama and art morning. In the drama session, our pupils lead the morning and they produce a piece of drama around the chosen books. The artwork they produce is also excellent, and that is displayed in the local library. Our fourth visit is to the central junior library where the librarians organize activities around the chosen books. On a final visit, we make presentations to pupils for their contributions. All the boys massively enjoy the responsibility they are given in this whole process and there is no doubt their perceptions of books and reading has significantly improved.

Application

Boys like books that are in a series:

Artemis Fowl, *Young Bond*, *Captain Underpants*, *His Dark Materials*, *Series of Unfortunate Events*, *Mortal Engines*, *Edge Chronicles*, *Windsinger*, *Narnia*, *Lord of the Rings*.

Boys like books that have an edge to them:

Weirdo's War, *Creeper*, *Jake's Tower*, *Martyn Pig*, *The Crew*, *Boy Kills Man*; and works by authors like Benjamin Zephaniah, Anthony Horowitz, Malorie Blackman and Bali Rai.

Boys like books that are about powerful ideas:

Bloodtide, *Millions*, *I am the Cheese*, *Warriors of the Raven*, *Wheel of Fire*, *Feather Boy*; and works by authors such as Keith Gray, David Almond and Philip Pullman.

Boys like books that draw on myth, legend and fantasy:

The Wizard of Earthsea, *Keys to the Kingdom*, *Beowulf*, Arthurian legends and Norse sagas; and works by authors such as Alan Garner, Susan Cooper, D. Wynne Jones, Christopher Paolini and Peter Dickinson.

Boys like books that appeal to their sense of mischief:

The Legend of Spud Murphy, *Horrid Henry*, *Jiggy McQue*; and by writers such as Roald Dahl, Terry Pratchett, Roddy Doyle, Maurice Gleitzman, Jeremy Strong, Ian Ogilvy, Philip Ridley and Louis Sachar.

Boys like books that are funny:

The Discworld series, Jiggy stories, Adrian Mole, Little Wolf stories, Joey Pigza stories, Justin, Just William, Jennings; and books by writers such as Douglas Adams, Philip Ardagh, Paul Jennings and Pete Johnson.

Boys like books that are plot driven:

Harry Potter, *Holes*, *Eagle of the Ninth*, *Stravaganza*, *Hatchet*, *Abhorsen*, *Sharpe*; and books by writers such as Theresa Breslin, Cornelia Funke, Charlie Higson, Conn Iggulden, Robert Swindells, Graham Joyce, Jonathan Stroud, Caroline Lawrence, Robert Muchamore, Keith Oppel, Chris Ryan, Darren Shan.

Collected by the author from 200 children's library service workers at their annual conference in 2006, using a series of mind maps. Many books and authors could of course have appeared in more than one category.

Concept

Boys and literacy checklist 1

I currently provide a sense of purpose and audience in my subject area when...	I may now consider
I currently supply support with planning and preparation when...	I may now consider
I currently link talk and writing when...	I may now consider
I currently use the following to help develop skills to structure...	I may now consider
I currently chunk up written work in the following ways...	I may now consider

Boys and literacy checklist 2

I currently provide the following opportunities to reflect...	I may now consider
I currently respond to written work by...	I may now consider
I currently use the following approaches to encourage and develop boys' pride in their work...	I may now consider
I currently provide the following opportunities for 'speaking and listening activities without a catch!'...	I may now consider
I currently use the following strategies to encourage boys to read...	I may now consider

Classroom practice

Concept

Barrier 8 **Mismatch in teaching and learning styles**

The lives of four- and five-year-old boys are filled with storybook characters and associated merchandise, cartoons and superheroes on television, in comics, on their lunchboxes, on pencil cases, on their bedroom walls – so why not in their classrooms? Despite their worst fears – for example, that it may lead to more boisterous behaviour – early years practitioners have been amazed at the positive outcomes, most notably the complete lack of violence and 'macho' behaviour. Instead, what has been noted has been an unleashing of the imagination, a subsequent improved ability to develop narrative and a startling ability to play co-operatively. Janet Paley, a leading exponent of what she terms 'Superhero Play', claims:

> Through fantasy play, children are able to use intuitive language, express themselves, gain pleasure, develop curiosity and express feelings and fears.

One basic approach of this activity is to allow all the boys to wear (non-descript) cloaks all day. What commonly develops is that girls soon want in on the action, any role plays start to develop caring elements, and children begin to work co-operatively together to create huge models and fantastical narratives. Other approaches, such as the Steiner School, which engages pupils in using natural materials, can also be seen to be reflecting many boys' interests and preferred ways of working. The same can also be said of the Danish Forest Schools, which encourage more time spent outdoors. The Emiglio School in Italy de-emphasizes literacy skills until boys are ready and each has a resident artist who they refer to as their 'mad uncle'. All these approaches are now influencing a growing number of early years' settings.

The need for boys to improve their ability to reflect is well understood and this section provides a wide range of ideas to build in opportunities for reflection. This section also provides practical suggestions to improve boys' learning by considering appropriate seating, pupil grouping and effective group-work strategies.

Application

Learning cycle checklist

The four-stage learning cycle shown below does hit all the right buttons for boys without disadvantaging girls, simply because it is *good practice*.

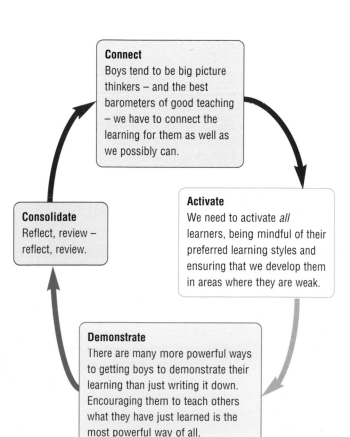

Connect
Boys tend to be big picture thinkers – and the best barometers of good teaching – we have to connect the learning for them as well as we possibly can.

Activate
We need to activate *all* learners, being mindful of their preferred learning styles and ensuring that we develop them in areas where they are weak.

Demonstrate
There are many more powerful ways to getting boys to demonstrate their learning than just writing it down. Encouraging them to teach others what they have just learned is the most powerful way of all.

Consolidate
Reflect, review – reflect, review.

Concept

There are several health warnings attached to teaching and learning styles. To begin with, we cannot say that all boys are kinesthetic learners with anywhere near the same amount of certainty that we can say that the vast majority of teachers have a marked preference for visual modes of learning. This amounts, in my experience, to at least 90 per cent of primary teachers, but probably around 10 per cent fewer on average in high schools. What we can say, however, is that a significant number of the boys we are concerned about do demonstrate, for a large amount of their time in school, a preference for kinesthetic learning. When you consider that we tend to teach in the way we learn best, the potential for a mismatch is obvious. As teaching and learning styles pioneer Barbara Prashnig says, when we ask a lot of boys to follow our rules – 'Sit still', 'Stop fiddling' and 'Stop chewing' – we are often saying to the active boy, who is also highly tactile and in need of lots of intake (pens, gum and so on), 'Stop learning!'

The second major health warning with regard to the learning styles debate is that education is not about identifying a child's preferred learning style and then teaching children in that particular mode forever. It is about balance, and ensuring that we teach all children to their strengths while at the same time developing other areas to create well-rounded learners.

I would also add that without the right environment for learning, no learning can take place regardless of how it is delivered.

> **TIP:**
> Barbara Prashnig states that preferred teaching styles can and should be used to their very best effect when new and difficult information is being taught and when pupils are studying for exams.

Application

What do you do already and what might you consider?

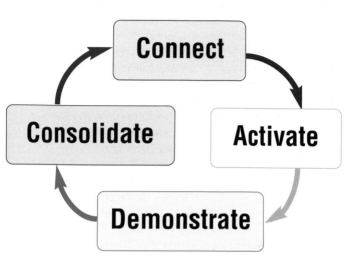

As a group, using an enlarged version of the above diagram, share
your ideas for each of the four elements of the learning cycle.

Concept

Barrier 9 **Lack of opportunities for reflection**

Kolb's learning cycle (below) is a widely recognized model of how we learn. Looking at this model we can say that, unquestionably, the weakest aspect of many boys' learning process is their inability to reflect. Instead, many want to move straight on to the next activity, without wanting to even pause for breath. The boy charging around the primary playground while the girls are heavily involved in conversation, or the boy who is furiously flicking from one page to another in the 'Whoppinggreatbigbookofrecords' while many girls are sat around lost in a world of a wonderful story invariably becomes the boy who cannot write that written evaluation at the age of 16 for his design and technology coursework. He may even become the man who can never open up and express his feelings. Many boys' ability and often the desire to slow down the pace and reflect are frequently sorely missing. The process needs to begin early and perhaps we need to think a little more imaginatively if we wish to make significant changes.

The worst case scenario for boys can significantly reduce their ability to learn. For example, if plenaries are insufficiently used, then for many boys this can be hugely disadvantageous, since, as Mike Hughes would say, 'Trying to learn without reviewing is like trying to fill the bath without putting the plug in.' In question-and-answer sessions, if pupils are not encouraged to reflect with a partner before answering but are instead encouraged to just stick their hands up, then a few boys may have a go at exhibiting their wonderful risk-taking behaviour, while another group will simply think of something else to do because they can't be bothered to even think, let alone participate. Again limited reflection has taken place.

1. Personal experience
2. Reflection & synthesis
3. New ideas, greater understanding
4. Testing

Application

- ■ 'Tummy time' – early years' children lie in a circle, heads on chins, talking about what they have been doing.
- ■ 'Lovely eyes' – engage with one early years' child one-to-one: 'show me those lovely eyes'.
- ■ Visualizations – these can be used to create a sense of peace, mentally rehearse and prepare for pressurized situations, take a journey into nature, engage with and deal with fears and even set intentions for the day that will engage the law of attraction.
- ■ Meditation – there are many and varied techniques that specifically aid the ability to reflect.
- ■ Simple yoga, basic Tai Chi and breathwork – these invariably lead into meditation and contemplation.
- ■ Circle time – used extensively in primary schools, yet barely used at all in secondary schools.
- ■ Philosophy for Children (P4C) – use collaborative, creative, critical and caring thinking skills in the context of a community of enquiry.
- ■ Questioning – encourage student questioning student.
- ■ No hands up zones – work with partners in question-and-answer sessions: give them three minutes to think of three answers.
- ■ Think–pair–share – think about an idea, discuss it with a partner and share it with the class.
- ■ Diaries or planners – introduce reflection diaries or modify school planners to incorporate space for written reflections.

Concept

It can be at critical times that reflection skills are called upon and boys are very often found wanting. As with the design technology coursework that suddenly calls upon him to recall and reflect upon two years' work at what seems like the drop of a hat, solutions such as an ongoing reflective diary can prove useful. Sydney Stringer High School expanded this idea across the whole curriculum in order to sharpen up boys' reflective skills. A 'Learning diary' that they initially designed was to encourage their boys to reflect upon precisely what it was that they had learned. Specifically, they were asked to identify three different things they had learned in any given lesson.

To begin with, teachers noted that boys just simply listed what they had done. In conversation, it transpired that most of the boys were actually unclear about what it was they had actually learned. The diaries were subsequently modified in collaboration with the boys, and the boys were gradually moulded into a way of thinking around what learning had taken place, what mistakes they were making and how improvements could be made. The process also significantly altered teachers' perceptions of their own teaching and learning with one of the designers of the scheme declaring: 'It certainly made me begin to focus more on my plenary!'

Other schools such as Mitchell School in Stoke on Trent supply all pupils with a reflective diary in order to record any thoughts throughout the school day on experiences and feelings, challenges and rewards.

As for the classroom, moments of reflection such as the plenary are the most important part of the lesson, but the plenary is not just for Christmas! It's for any time. We have to go for **multiplenaries**! All children need time to review their learning frequently. Most boys **desperately** need to.

Application

- Talking partners/reflective partners – discuss 'time out' questions that can be displayed around the room such as 'How does this link with something we've done in another subject?' 'How are we going to remember this?' 'Where is this lesson leading us?'
- Produce a graphic representation of what has been learned such as a mind map, plus and minus interesting factors (PMI), Venn diagram, flow chart and so on.
- Reflection relay – as in a team relay race, pupils take it in turns to add to a sheet something they have learned that lesson.
- 3–2–1 – students say what are the three most important things they have learned, what two things are still unclear and one way in which they can connect what they have just learned with something they have learned previously.
- Hot seat students as 'learning experts'.
- At mid-lesson all learners are asked to stand and imagine they are on the tube, hanging onto the strap – it is busy. They strike up a conversation with a neighbouring passenger about what they have just learned at school.
- Create a display of digital photographs of different activities in the lesson, display at the end of the lesson and ask students to describe what learning was taking place.
- Students mime key ideas from the lesson as outrageously as possible.
- Learners produce a piece of movement and rap that represents a definition of key terms from the lesson.
- 'Big Brother diary' – allow free comments on their learning whenever they choose during the lesson, onto a digital video camera. Watch unedited footage at the end.

Concept

Barrier 10 **Inappropriate student grouping**

It is my belief that setting is one of the most significant barriers to boys' achievement. In a school that strictly sets, no one wants to teach the bottom set Year 8 humanities group on Friday afternoon. Why? Because they are made up largely of disaffected boys who have been told they are no good. We can persist in telling them that they are in a flexible situation (invariably they are not), but for how long will they believe in that – or in themselves? Not long. How much longer must we continue in education to be so arrogant as to think that young people learn only from adults, or that it is OK to put the linguistically most deprived in the linguistically most deprived environment?

The above sentiments appeared in *Breaking through Barriers to Boys' Achievement*, and shortly thereafter I was described in *The Guardian* newspaper as one of the country's most articulate opponents of setting. I was flattered but I disagree with the description. The bottom set boys I speak to on a regular basis are far more articulate about what it means to them. We are hugely aware that peer groups are at least as influential in a child's development as families, yet we continue to create and perpetuate groups that can generate huge areas of disaffection in our schools. It is absolutely clear that for many their sense of self-worth as learners, so inextricably linked with their developing self-esteem, is invariably extremely low. Has *your school* ever asked students how they feel about the grouping that it insists upon?

One approach to student grouping that has been receiving attention of late is single-sex grouping in order to raise boys' achievement. There is virtually no evidence at all to suggest that this has real benefits for boys; indeed, the evidence is far more compelling that while girls often benefit, boys' groups tend to develop more 'laddish' tendencies. The latter is exactly what we do not need.

Application

Discussion cards

A parent at a parents' evening tells you that at school he was in bottom sets for every subject and it was eight years after leaving school before he started to think that he was any good at anything. Now his son is in the same position in school – demotivated and with very low aspirations. How do you assure him that setting is in his son's best interest?

A parent brings in a snippet from a newspaper that refers to research that shows that setting actually benefits no one. Explain to this parent why it is that you are convinced otherwise.

Your school opts for boys-only groups in your subject area as an experiment. A senior manager observes one of the lessons and notes that the head of department has deployed the best male teacher to work with them. He also notes that the relationship between teacher and boys now revolves around significant 'laddish banter'. How does your department support such a move?

You are aware that in your particular subject, top sets are predominantly made up of girls while bottom sets are predominantly made up of boys. As a department, you decide that you need to look at alternatives. What might you consider?

hy not interview a number of 'bottom set boys' about their
ws of their situation. Then get them to interview you about what
ng is all about.

Concept

Barrier 11 Inappropriate seating arrangements

Schools need to proactively consider seating arrangements in the classroom in order to assist raising boys' achievement, not least since, given free rein, the naughtiest boys will sit on the teacher's right at the very back. The next 'rank' will be along the sides, just outside the teacher's peripheral vision. There are schools where seating policies exist making boy–girl seating obligatory. I believe that there are fundamental problems with this approach. Logistically, in 'setted' situations, you run out of boys in top sets and girls in bottom sets! In other situations, where a gender imbalance exists, girls are often allowed to sit next to girls but boys are not allowed to sit together. These premises appear to be an attempt to civilize the boy with a girl's presence and to ensure that boys learn many skills that come more readily to girls such as empathy and that girls in turn learn skills such as assertiveness from boys. How frequently do observers of such arrangements actually see this kind of cross-pollination taking place? How much more frequently do we see disgruntled pupils and the development of further 'learned helplessness' in boys? Asking students how they feel in this situation (which I highly recommend), eight- and nine-year-old boys have told me they liked working with girls because: 'They do all the work' and 'They tell you all the answers'. Girls have told me: 'Sometimes I don't like working with boys because they act stupid' and 'They don't go along with what you're doing, they just daydream.' A group of Year 10 boys recently told me their top two reasons for liking sitting next to girls were that they could copy their work and 'feel their leg' – not the greatest of educational outcomes for this basically unjust and ill-considered strategy.

Application

Getting seating right in classrooms is vital, and there are a range of criteria and strategies to consider. Flexibility is fundamentally important. At different times boys will benefit from sitting with their friends, with girls and with people they would never normally choose.

Which of these have you used seating plans for?

- Encouraging peer support.
- Encouraging language development.
- Encouraging the sharing of different skills or consolidating shared expertise.
- Inhibiting peer pressure, sexual harassment, bullying and intimidation.
- Combining students with shared preferred learning styles for revision purposes.
- Combining students with shared preferred learning styles for learning new and difficult materials.
- Allowing for personal preferences with regard to the levels of lighting and types of seating.
- Addressing specific difficulties – such as those with spelling problems to the front-left of the teacher.

Consider also:

- Seating plans are vital when supply teachers take a class.
- Seating plans can be displayed (and readily amended) on a smartboard.

Concept

Barrier 12 **Ineffective group-work**

Flexibility of student grouping in your classroom means that sometimes you put together groups whose members have different skills, or are clearly capable of helping others in the group, or share the same learning style or share the same interest. But is there ever a place for ability groups? Personally, I do not believe there is. It might be argued that when group-work is set up appropriately, the benefits for the group members are not dissimilar to the benefits that accrue from mixed ability classes:

> Less heterogeneous groupings are especially advantageous for medium ability students. When students of the same ability are grouped together, it has been found that high ability students thought it unnecessary to help one another while low ability students were less able to do so.

(Askew and Wiliam, 1995)

A clear set of criteria for grouping in order to gain maximum engagement from boys, needs to be accompanied by a very clear sense of purpose, a clearly defined task and, to improve matters even more, a very clearly defined set of roles for each member of the group.

Group-work, when established effectively, can be of particular value to boys. Circle time, for example, is used in virtually every primary school in the UK and some high schools, most commonly in lower school PSHCE. It is all about listening to each other, valuing opinions and developing self-esteem. P4C is an engaging, structured and purposeful approach to group-work with added boy appeal because of the challenge/competitive element and, often, the hint of status that its title conveys. Massively useful for boys in terms of building self-esteem, and developing them as more reflective and considerate human beings (see page 47).

Application

- 'Hot potato' thinking skills activity – each group member has a clearly defined role and the task is simple but extremely focused. The time-limited nature of the activity adds to its success with boys (see page 88).

- Delegation – set up resource centres around the room such as a video, pages of a textbook, a PowerPoint presentation, an internet site, a cassette to listen to. Each home group sends a delegate to a resource centre to discover what is available. Delegates at the bases help each other interpret the information within a time limit then return to base to collate information (Ginnis, 2001).

- Jigsaw – subject under study is divided into chunks. In groups, each pupil studies a chunk of the given information with a specific task. Individual members of every group who have studied the same chunk come together as a group of experts to work on their common task. Ultimately, each pupil returns to the home group to share their expertise, together building up a whole picture. A major task is then set which requires the use of everyone's new expertise. Purposeful, engaging *and* involving getting around the classroom.

- Simple as … ABC – A=explainer, B=Questioner, C=Reporter. A explains something they have learned while B prompts them for more information and C notes how they do and reports back.

Concept

Barrier 13 **Mismatch in assessment and boys' preferred ways of working**

How familiar is Nathan's story, whose behaviour, the teacher had determined, was typical of a boy? Nathan in his apparently blasé way had been saying for week after week that he had left his coursework at home. This was excused, albeit reluctantly, by his teacher who saw this as being 'boys' terrible organizational ability'. From time to time, he half-heartedly scrawled a few, largely irrelevant bits and pieces on paper whenever he was given time for coursework in class. January in Year 11 arrived and inevitably a point came when Nathan felt not only overwhelmed by the size of the task but also total confusion, as he had not kept a clear picture in his head of what the coursework should look like at that stage or, indeed, where it was ultimately going. Fear of looking stupid in front of his teacher by breaking the habit of a lifetime and asking or by bringing in a piece of work that was totally inadequate, he had two choices – fail or seek help elsewhere. In his case he was lucky, the school had a number of learning mentors and he received support and time from an adult who appeared to desperately care about him. This particular Nathan, estimated grade E in September, actually received a grade A. Many, many more do not.

It is now clearly understood that, generally, a large number of boys fare better and feel happier with examinations, which suit their risk-taking behaviour, rather than the long-term nature of coursework, which contains many elements that are not particularly friendly – not least the business of hugely deferred gratification and the demands of long-term planning and organization. There are certain key elements of coursework that cause particular problems. Many strategies can and have been tried very successfully.

Application

Boys and coursework

■ *Boy-friendly chunks or working in chapters*

Establishing a set of criteria for a small section at a time, setting short-term goals and a series of realistic deadlines. As soon as is practicable, each chapter is returned with quality feedback.

■ *Reflective diary*

Expecting many boys to produce an evaluation 'cold' at the end of a two-year course, for example, can often be immensely challenging for them. The unreasonable request, as it appears to many, that they draw together all the 'threads' and contemplate their successes and otherwise over the previous two years can and should be eased by the introduction of a reflective journal. In design technology, for example, this would include keeping an ongoing record of their experience, feelings and observations at each step along the way.

■ *Organization*

Not allowing coursework to be taken home can be a very simple and often very effective approach, as can rewarding completion of each step. We often delude ourselves that by Year 11, boys have outgrown rewards – not so.

■ *Seeing the big picture*

- A mind map of what elements a finished piece of coursework should contain.
- An effective contents grid on a coursework folder cover, incorporating a very graphic element that is filled in as work progresses – such as a pie chart, jigsaw or graph.
- Exemplars on display. 'I wouldn't have known what an A* looked like if I hadn't seen that' (see page 72).

Change the system – or change syllabus!

At the time of writing, there is (again) in the UK talk of changing back from coursework to examinations – not for the educational benefits this may have for boys, by creating a more level playing field, but to stop cheating. If only! Some boards do offer different proportions of coursework and we are all free to choose. Ironically, some English departments are currently switching to the Welsh Board because of a very positive coursework element. It provides the ability to deal with a hugely complex array of poetry in a quickly delivered 'chunk' of coursework rather than expect boys to draw together the threads of information together from over a long period of time.

Emotional intelligence

4

Concept

Barriers 14 Emotional intelligence issues

If we teach our sons to honor and value their emotional lives, if we can give boys an emotional vocabulary and the encouragement to use it, they will unclench their hearts.

(Kindlon and Thompson, 1999)

Girls, according to one study, are six times more likely to use the word 'love', but just as likely to use the word 'mad'. Why? Because two emotions that parents will actually talk about with boys from when they are very young are fear and anger. Boys are actively discouraged, not only in their speech but also in their actions, from expressing many emotions at all. 'Pull yourself together!' 'Don't be so soft!' 'Wimp!' 'Wuss!' The need to honour boys' tender feelings is a huge issue that parents, and teachers, must constantly address.

Studies show very clearly, for example, that mothers who talk more about emotional responses and who do not respond negatively to outward displays of fear, anger, sadness and so on, end up with children who are far more literate emotionally. More often than not it is older males who tend to perpetuate gender stereotypes in younger boys. Within schools, this is the reason why we need teachers who portray models of caring masculinity, not least because the teaching of emotional intelligence means beginning with ourselves. As far as boys are concerned, work on emotional intelligence is not just a good idea, it is fundamentally important. To this end, we can now celebrate the delivery into schools of support materials designed to provide for work on self-awareness, emotional control, self-motivation, empathy and handling relationships.

Application

Me?

Sing, me?
Dance?
Violin me?
No chance

Act, me?
Paint?
Arty type?
I ain't

Write, me?
Poetry?
Like me?
Not likely

Read me?
Books?
Brain food?
Get stuffed

Think me?
Think not

Care, me?
Go away
Scared, me?
NO WAY

Love, me?
Squeeze?
Hold me?

…please

Gary Wilson

Use the above as the stimulus for a P4C session as follows:

- Ensure participants understand fully the difference between a shallow question and a deep, philosophical question that will take them on an interesting journey of exploration.
- Allow a few minutes for everyone to come up with a deep question in silence.
- Ask participants to share their question with a partner.
- After a few minutes, ask them to decide which of their two questions is the best – they may combine their questions if they wish.
- Write up each question, valuing everyone's contribution and asking if anyone needs clarification.
- Participants vote for the very best question.
- The community of enquiry begins and participants can join in with openings such as 'I agree with … because' or 'I disagree with … because' or 'Could you please explain what you mean by…' or 'Actually I disagree with all of you, what I think is…'

Much of the visual material and many of the dilemmas in SEAL materials are also well suited to this approach.

Concept

Across the country, there are numerous other examples of practical approaches to developing emotional intelligence within and outside the curriculum, including training young people in counselling skills and mediation skills, establishing 'Buddy Schemes' and 'Befrienders', and providing anger management classes. An audit of what currently takes place where you are would be a very good place to start. One of the most common examples in terms of developing self-awareness and emotional control has to be drama, which can reach all the parts that other subjects cannot. Drama techniques across the curriculum can open up more than just a tricky concept within a subject lesson.

I like drama because it gives me lots of words I never knew I had.

Year 8 boy

In terms of self-motivation, for example, Tupton Hall School was aware of the number of Year 11 boys who were totally demotivated and, to all intents and purpose, invisible. In order to make these boys believe they could achieve, the school started giving them motivation scores. The boys genuinely failed to understand why they scored so poorly. Once their teachers had mimicked their behaviours back to them (in a good-natured way of course!), explaining what physiology said about motivation, they began to understand and rapidly moved on.

It is well understood that most girls and women are far more empathic than most males, and numerous school projects focus very directly on this area. A group of boys in desperate need of mentoring were taken by their mentors on a regular basis to a local old people's home to talk to and offer help to the residents. Teenagers and Toddlers, a project to combat teenage pregnancy, engages older boys deemed to be at risk to work with toddlers with special needs.

We need to continue to find more and more opportunities to enhance the development of emotional intelligence. It may even help if we actively reward and celebrate far more the achievements related to developing emotional intelligence than we do those other achievements the system is so often totally preoccupied with.

Application

Beyond the SEALs

It is not the intention of SEAL (Social and Emotional Aspects of Learning) materials to provide for ALL teaching and learning around emotional intelligence. Indeed, there are clearly many ways to supplement the delivery of the work. Vital Connections, for example, working with Goleman's 'S.E.R.I.O.U.S. model' show how a holistic approach can enhance it wonderfully.

Self-motivation – 'do-in' (Japanese movement exercises)
Empathy – peer massage
Reflection – meditation, quiet space, visualization
Impulse control – Yoga and Chi Kung
Optimism – positive affirmations
Understanding relationships – positive touch and the philosophy of yoga
Self-awareness – breath work

Consider with colleagues other complimentary ideas from the curriculum or beyond.

SEALs: the five key areas	Definition	Your complementary ideas
Self-awareness	The capacity to recognize your feelings as they happen	
Emotional control	The ability to manage your emotional reactions, control impulses and recover from life's upsets	
Self-motivation	The ability to use the emotions to pursue a goal, staying hopeful, even in the face of setbacks	
?pathy	Emotional sensitivity to other people's feelings	
?ng ?hips	Encompassing social skills such as leadership, teamwork and confidence in dealing with other people	

Concept

Barrier 15 Low self-esteem and limiting self-beliefs

It is said that we use up to three times more energy worrying about doing something than actually doing it. For those underachieving boys with low self-esteem, the effort of exercising those limiting self-beliefs mean that many look completely exhausted with the effort of getting nowhere! Their physiology is often in a state of a permanent slump! Why is this? A significant element is their inner voice. According to Learning Styles pioneer Barbara Prashnig, the inner voice (or the internal auditory as she refers to it) of underachieving boys is 'huge'. You might engender interesting discussion with the question, 'Would you talk to your friends the way you sometimes talk to yourself?' You could ask them what they hold onto longer, a criticism or a compliment. Invariably, as with most of us, the answer will be the former. So how do we change their internal voices from negative to positive? We could begin by asking what it is that is so burdensome in their heads that it means that their faces are almost permanently facing the ground. We could ask them about the weight they have been carrying so long that has created their permanently slumped shoulders.

Jack Canfield, author of *Chicken Soup for the Soul* (2000), would say to anyone at this point, having unburdened their story, 'So what? What are you going to focus on NOW!'

We could ask where they would actually like to be and then send them on that journey in their hearts and minds, and make it feel so powerfully, irresistibly real that they focus on that and nothing else, ultimately reaching their goal.

Application

Generate the feeling of how it will feel to do well in your next test. First of all, find a place to be perfectly still and away from any disturbance.

- CLOSE YOUR EYES.
- ACT AS IF the day has arrived and you wake up smiling. Feel the muscles in your face stretch into a smile. Put on your favourite music.
- ACT AS IF you are sitting down for a lovely breakfast, it's a real treat. Tasty yes?
- ACT AS IF you pick up your bag, walk out of the door. Feel that bounce in your step as your feet hit the pavement.
- ACT AS IF you enter the examination room and sit down, upright and eager. Feel the rim of your chair as you lift it and yourself closer to the table.
- ACT AS IF you are leafing through the paper, calmly, and with a growing sense of well-being and confidence. Hear yourself saying, 'That's not a problem' 'I know that' 'That one's easy!'
- ACT AS IF you calmly and purposefully begin to write. The pen feels comfortable in your hand and the words flow out onto the page.
- ACT AS IF you are taking out just a few minutes to breathe deeply and stretch between questions. Feel the difference.
- FEEL THE JOY as your last word is committed to paper. Make that final full stop.
- FEEL THE JOY as you return home, throw your bag on the bed and congratulate yourself on a job well done. Put on your favourite music.

Concept

We could introduce them to these ideas and in this way release so much potential. So why don't we? It could be because we need to get rid of those inner voices that are currently saying:

- 'There's no way I could get involved in that kind of stuff.'
- 'It's not my area of expertise.'
- 'Even if I did believe in all that stuff, the kids would just laugh at me.'
- 'Besides, it won't work anyway!'
- 'Some of these boys will just never get it!'

And so on and so on. Perhaps we need to first of all experience how it works for ourselves. In that case, try out the 'Application' elements for yourself first.

Consider this: scientists tracked the brain patterns and the muscle movements of a number of Olympic athletes as they visualized running a race that they had run previously. Signals in the brain relayed to the muscles meant that exactly the same muscles fired in precisely the same sequence during the visualization of the race as had been fired during the real event. The brain cannot tell the difference between really doing something and visualizing doing it. In much the same way, the brain has the power to create many elements of an experience before we actually experience it. If we create it in a positive way before we experience it, just think of the impact on that limiting self-belief that is currently writing the script for these boys, or you!

It is well understood that we use a tiny proportion of our mind's potential, it would appear that for the first time in our history there is a growing movement and a deepening understanding of how we can significantly unleash far more

Whatever the mind can conceive, it can achieve.

W. Clement Sto

Application

Positive affirmations: student prompt sheet

Your parents may have experienced it, buying a new car, suddenly thousands of other people had the same model, suddenly all of these cars had come into their reality because they had been focusing on that particular model whereas previously they had not.

Constantly saying 'I don't want to fail in my next maths assessment' means that you probably will! Why? Because you are focusing on failure and maths. Whatever you tend to focus on will tend to show up. It's called the law of attraction. Focusing positively can attract positive results. Positive affirmations have been understood for centuries as a very real way of lifting your self-confidence, banishing limiting self-beliefs and improving performance.

You must, however, follow a simple set of rules.

- The affirmation must be written in the present tense, 'I am now working brilliantly and I am…'.
- The affirmation must contain only *what you want* and *not* what you don't want.
- You must get into the *feeling* of how it will be. Display it prominently in your room and refer to it regularly, repeating it to yourself and print it on a small card to carry around so that you see it regularly. If it helps, think of this as programming your own internal computer with a programme that only plays positively.

Try this exercise with your class:

- Ask everyone to stand, feet together and arms by their sides.
- Ask them to raise one arm parallel to their shoulder, and point straight ahead.
- Ask them to keep their feet still but move their pointed arm to the right, as far as they can go, then note where they pointed to on the wall behind them.
- Ask them to remain in the same position but this time close their eyes and just *imagine* that they are repeating the exercise. 'Imagine that you are moving your arm round to the right, a bit further, a little bit further, and then instead of stopping, you carry on. In fact … you end up round the front. Unbelievable!' Ask them to *imagine* the process once more.

    Ask them to open their eyes and then repeat the actual process, noting where they reach the second time. Everyone will get further.

Concept

Barrier 16 **Teacher talk, teacher expectations**

In terms of teacher expectations, we all understand the power of the self-fulfilling prophecy. A school I worked with recently was anticipating (with dread) amalgamation with a nearby boys' school, starting with one year group. A term ahead of their arrival, they were already referring to them as 'nine Hell'. We spent some time talking about how maybe if we changed the language, we might change attitudes (staff and learners) and, subsequently, their performance. At the opposite end of the scale, I heard recently of a maths teacher who was called in by her head of department to explain why her set four group (largely boys) had done significantly better than the set two group in their exams. She apologized – she thought she had been teaching set two!

What happens all too frequently is that negative stereotyping of boys often masks their true potential. If our perceptions of them are as effective learners, then undoubtedly that is what they will become.

In virtually every single one of my conversations with groups of boys over the years, it is abundantly clear that boys firmly believe that teachers prefer girls. They often cite this as the number one reason why boys underperform. In actuality, the truth is that most teachers prefer boys because of their humour, their enthusiasm once they are running with something, their energy, directness and their risk-taking behaviour, which is seen to be challenging and refreshing. However, the traits that we mostly praise and actively encourage tend to be those most often exemplified by most of the girls in our classrooms such as neatness, compliance, adherence to task, good listening and so on.

You **love** boys! Show them that you do!

Application

Monitoring your interactions

In class, do you celebrate the kinds of 'boy behaviour' you know that you admire? Or do you ignore it, actively discourage it or even put them down for it? Monitoring your interactions with boys and girls can be extremely revealing. If the following seems too daunting a list to hand to a colleague to monitor and observe you with, you could always video yourself!

	Positive ☑	Negative ☒
Frequency and nature of interactions with boys **Notable phrases used**	☐ ☐ ☐ ☐ ☐ ☐ ☐ ☐ ☐ ☐ ☐ ☐ ☐ ☐ ☐	☐ ☐ ☐ ☐ ☐ ☐ ☐ ☐ ☐ ☐ ☐ ☐ ☐ ☐ ☐
Frequency and nature of interactions with girls **Notable phrases used**	☐ ☐ ☐ ☐ ☐ ☐ ☐ ☐ ☐ ☐ ☐ ☐ ☐ ☐ ☐	☐ ☐ ☐ ☐ ☐ ☐ ☐ ☐ ☐ ☐ ☐ ☐ ☐ ☐ ☐
Examples of boys' behaviours	How they were dealt with: positive	How they were dealt with: negative
Risk taking: _____	_____ _____	_____ _____
Liveliness: _____	_____ _____	_____ _____
Humour: _____	_____ _____	_____ _____
Directness: _____	_____ _____	_____ _____
·d and wonderful	_____ _____	_____ _____

Concept

One of the main reasons that boys believe teachers prefer girls is because of the ways in which they are spoken to. There is little doubt in my mind that we talk to boys and girls differently, and while many boys may not show it, because being a boy does not allow for that kind of thing, it hurts. It hurts more deeply than we may ever understand.

Talking to boys appropriately shows them respect. If they cannot get it from you, then they will attempt to get it from whoever they can, and that usually means their peers – and we know what behaviour that often leads to. I watched a teacher taking a class full of very challenging boys recently. She showed them the utmost respect and she was politeness itself. She expected – and received – the same by return. Her words of instruction were also words of encouragement:

- 'If you write nothing, it must be wrong. If you have a go, you may be right.'
- 'Saying you don't get it means you won't.'
- 'Before you ask (as one boy's impatient hand shoots in the air, seconds after a task is set), have you written the question yet and thought about what we did last lesson?' Boy, 'But I was away last lesson!' Teacher (quick as a flash), 'Well, why not have a go? Get it right today and you'll be doing really well won't you?' He did, and he felt really good about it.

It is now well understood that students will forget what you do and what you say, but they will never forget how you made them feel. There is no place in classrooms for:

- sarcasm
- put downs
- barbed comments
- turning your back on students
- interrupting students
- denigrating ideas or appearance.

Application

- Fasten a copy of the quote below behind all toilet doors in your staffroom.

> I am the decisive element in the classroom. It is my personal approach that creates the climate. It is my daily mood that makes the weather. As a teacher, I possess tremendous power to make a child's life miserable or joyous. I can be a tool of torture or an instrument of inspiration. I can humiliate or humour, hurt or heal. It is my response that decides whether a crisis will be escalated or de-escalated, a child humanised or dehumanised.
>
> (Ginott 1972)

- Try this exercise:

> Close your eyes (when you've finished reading!) and imagine a group of boys at the back of your classroom, misbehaving. It's Friday afternoon and you're trying to concentrate on getting through the lesson … What are you going to say? … Close your eyes … think … BOYS! The same lesson … it's a group of girls misbehaving … getting on your nerves … what are you going to say? … Close your eyes … think … GIRLS … Notice a difference?
>
> If we're not careful we use 'boys!' as a swear word!

- Try these three approaches for a month and see if you notice any difference.
    - **Say:** 'When I look at you I see someone who is capable of so much, someone who…'
    - **Say:** 'When you speak to me like that it makes me feel…' instead of 'Don't you speak to me like that!'
    - **Say:** 'Thank you' when you give an instruction – the assumption that it will be done often means that it will.

Concept

Barrier 17 Peer pressure

Peer pressure is, I believe, one of the most significant barriers to boys' achievement. Many boys happily sail through school immune to peer pressure if they are also good at sport. An instant licence is granted them by the Peer Police, since they are able to be 'one of the lads' and achieve. The Peer Police begin their careers patrolling the boundaries of gender-approved behaviour in the nursery playground and start to wield fairly significant power by the time they reach the top end of primary schools, ensuring that by this time many boys are more concerned with their friends' approval rather than their teacher's. By Years 10 and 11, they are running our high schools.

If you are wise enough and lucky enough to get the Peer Police onboard as part of a mentoring group, a revision class, a drama production, a summer school, a community project, or even a discussion in the classroom, then it's all right for all the other boys to come on board too. A licence has been granted. The ability for boys to accept rewards and celebrate success is limited by the power of the Peer Police. Of great significance too, bearing in mind the potential of the affective side of the curriculum to develop a more caring masculinity, is the fact that the Peer Police very often patrol the boundaries with particular fervour around the expressive, creative and performing arts.

There is, however, one characteristic that these youngsters possess that we must tap into in order to neutralize their negative impact. They are all natural born leaders. I belie' that if we focus on fine-tuning those skills in a positive w there is *great* potential to transform the Peer Police int positive force for good.

A significant number of barriers to boys' achievement fall under this category, including the nature of the laddish culture in schools and the lack of parental awareness of what they can do to help. Strategies to counter one of the most significant factors – peer pressure – as well as strategies to engage parents are provided here.

Application

Transforming the Peer Police

1. Engage them in specific roles of responsibility, such as peer mentors, junior playleaders, befrienders.

2. Engage them in the promotion of positive learning behaviour, such as in posters (also see VIPs page 66).

3. Engage them in leadership courses.

'Learning to Lead' course: Nicholas Chamberlaine Technology College in Warwickshire

- Students are taught a range of leadership skills building through Years 8 and 9.
- They complete personal challenges.
- They design, deliver, evaluate and assess a group challenge to improve the lives of others in their school or wider community.

'I've seen students lead a county conference for young leaders, leading workshops about leadership, go to local businesses and discuss their ideas about leadership and motivation with managing directors and their shop-floor leaders. They have also been to the National College for School Leadership training teachers and students in how to set up and run leadership courses.'

(Graham Tyrer, Deputy Headteacher)

The scheme has been so successful, it has now been taken up by one in three Warwickshire schools.

Concept

Barrier 18 Laddish culture

There is little doubt that laddish behaviour clearly contributes to the problem of boy's achievement. It is not surprising, therefore, that limited attention seems to have been given towards its full array of manifestations. Could it be that there exists, even in educational institutions, a tacit agreement that 'boys will be boys' and that certain behaviours are therefore to be played down, dealt with lightly, ignored or even encouraged? In your school, is it the norm for boys to greet each other with a hefty blow to the shoulder? Is it the norm for boys to dominate discussions, call out, throw things? Is it the norm for boys to name call other boys because they work hard, because they appear more sensitive, because of their appearance, their supposed sexual prowess or orientation? Is it the norm for boys to use aggressive language towards each other in the corridor, in the playground, on the playing field or use abusive language against girls about their appearance or suggesting promiscuous behaviour?

The truth is that boys are not violent, loud, abusive, sexist and aggressive just because they are boys. Many are directed that way by society at large and often by parents whose own upbringing has reflected those models of sexuality fed by a diet of macho propaganda in the tabloids, in movies, in the street, in the pub and on the football terraces. With that to go home to, that leaves teachers as the only ones in a position to create change. In the light of many failures in the past, some of us may even be tempted to contemplate thinking outside the box. For example, try changing the culture of the corridor, providing sanctuary and introducing yoga and peer massage as ways of ameliorating the macho elements. Whatever you choose your expectations of their behaviour really matters – to make the change we have to be the change. Boys do not have to be *BOYS!*

Application

A shopping list

- Sexual harassment
- Homophobic bullying
- Anti-abusive language policy

As you contemplate the shopping list, you may wish to try the 'out of the box' strategy below devised by educationalist Susan Ainscough – it might just help to turn things around.

- Extend the arms together at chest level outwards as fists but with the thumbs exposed, keeping the arms soft at the joints and keeping elbows and wrists close together.
- Exhale as you draw the arms in towards the solar plexus and make a 'shhhhhhhhhh' sound.
- As you keep doing this, imagine that you are releasing old negative patterns.
- Repeat this six or seven times.
- Visualize in the mind's eye a hot air balloon – really see the colours and be aware of the texture.
- The day is perfect for ballooning – there is just the right breeze.
- As you gaze up at the sky, be aware of the space and feel a sense of elation and freedom at the prospect of ascending.
- Climb in!
- Surrounding you are heavy stones – these are like your tensions and limiting beliefs about yourself that can hold you back.
- To fly you have to release these heavy burdens.
- Maybe you can name them. 'Fear holds me back' – let that one go. 'What do my friends think?' – let that one go.
- The balloon can now rise and as it does, you feel free to be yourself – unafraid, confident and believing in yourself.
- As you glide on the current of air, you feel inspired and enthusiastic about life – unique, strong, powerful, wise, kind to yourself and others.
- Whatever you can dream, you can be it!
- Gradually, you should feel light, free, positive and strong, and know that you can choose how you react and behave.
- Feel the balloon slowly descend until you feel a soft thud as you reach the ground.
  Take your time to come back to the room and open new eyes that are confident and clear.

Concept

Barrier 19 The influence of street culture

Boys behaving anti-socially on the streets troubled Egyptian elders, according to ancient hieroglyphics. Ancient Greek and Roman towns and provinces were also troubled by such behaviour. The first hint of modern youth culture began to appear with the advent of the 'Scuttlers' and 'Peaky Blinders', who roamed the streets in Victorian England. Then there were the original hooligans in Ireland. 'Teenagers' first hit the scene in America in the 1940s, either hanging around the streets or riding around on motorbikes like the 'Wild One'. In England, mods and rockers took to the streets in the early 1960s often in seaside towns where they chose to riot. Beatniks, skinheads, hippies, punks, Goths, New Agers, Acid House Ravers and Chavs all followed on in fairly rapid succession. Not all movements were exclusively male of course, but many were predominantly so. Most of the modern movements spawned huge cultural explosions in music, dance, fashion and art. Much, if not all, of which has been traditionally ignored in the world of education.

One obvious question about street culture is, 'Why the street?' The answer is often because it is the only place to go, to be like you want to be and to do what you want to do. Many are drawn to it in the need to develop identity, a sense of belonging and excitement. Of course, there are negative aspects to the culture that many are drawn to. However, an acknowledgement that the music, dance, art, rap and so on that boys engage with is worthwhile or even exciting is an acknowledgement of a very significant part of their developing self-image. This may not only increase engagement with school, but also, for those who are tempted by the 'heavier' scene, fulfil another need – one safe engagement with street culture.

Application

Accentuate the positive

Imagine that 'street culture' is a rival firm that has opened up for business down the street and it is taking away all your customers. What is it offering your boys that you are not?

- A sense of identity?
- A sense of belonging?
- A feeling of security?
- Excitement?
- FUN?
- What are you going to do about it?

Begin by raising your own awareness of 'street' issues – talk to the boys. Get them to help you fill in the grid below.

Street ...	A place in school?
Art	
Dance	
Rap	
Music	
Fashion	
??	

Concept

Barrier 20 Lack of positive male role models

The lack of positive male role models in society is hugely unfortunate to say the least. During the last football world cup, for example, hugely anticipated by most boys the world over, boys saw their heroes skulking off pitches when substituted, like small children being called in for their teas. They saw cheating and diving and countless acts of violence, and one of the most significant perpetrators (Zinedine Zidane) seemingly exonerated of it entirely by being rewarded player of the tournament.

Increasingly, there are fewer and fewer adult males in the family home. The teaching profession is, meanwhile, becoming more and more female orientated with under 4 per cent of the current teaching profession being made up of men below the age of 30. Of great importance, too, is the lack of other significant males in the lives of adolescent boys in particular. Throughout history, societies all over the world have used males from outside the family in the initiation processes of boys into adulthood, such as the ancient traditions of native North Americans and tribal cultures in Africa. In the UK in modern times, youth clubs, youth groups, scouting, apprenticeships and so on continue to dwindle in number and with them the number of significant older males to help them in the process of initiation. For some, perhaps the closest they will come will be initiation through drug taking witnessed and encouraged by a group of their own peers.

Fundamental to this issue is trying to understand exactly what boys' ideas of role models are. Who do they look up to? What traits do they admire? Schools' ideas too are often limited: 'We've taken care of it – we've got photos in the library of their favourite footballers reading books.'

Application

Role models: the debate exploring student perceptions – student discussion cards

Who are your heroes in the media?
What is it that you like about them?

Does a hero have to be tough? Can you think of people who are heroic who you could never imagine being in a fight?

What does it mean to be brave?
Do you know anyone who is brave in unusual ways?

What is a 'real man'?

Do you ever hear sentences starting 'Real men don't…'? How do they end?

Can you think of anyone in the world who is a negative male role model?
List them with a partner.

What would you say are the best three characteristics of a positive male role model?

Can you name anyone from real life, anyone you know who answers that description?

Could you be on that list one day?
(The correct answer is YES!)

Concept

In *Breaking through Barriers to Boys' Achievement*, I refer to the significance of male PE teachers in high schools. If they present a tough male macho stereotype, then they can do a significant numbers of boys, those who cannot live up to this stereotype, a huge disfavour. In primary schools, it is not uncommon for parents to clamour excitedly for male teachers who will 'Do the discipline' and 'Run the football'. In both cases, I believe the answer to be the same – what all schools need are male teachers who model a caring masculinity. Those teachers are worth their weight in gold.

Case study: Stoke-on-Trent Sixth Form College

Engaging significant numbers of boys on a scheme to enthuse high school students about attending college has been hugely successful. The VIP scheme involves key students (boys and girls) as a 'Flying Squad', making presentations and delivering a 'rough guide' in high schools, making contributions to parents' evenings and admissions days, fundraising, forming a 'Green Team' and operating as peer mentors. The Principal cites those who appear to benefit most as boys who might themselves have been peer leaders who have been less than positive about education. For those boys in the high school who witness the 'turn around' of an ex-'dude', the message can be extremely potent. One measure of its success has been that the model has been emulated by one of the college's 'feeder' high schools, whose team operate within their partner primary schools generating enthusiasm and appeasing any fears of transition. Again, significant boys have adopted the role with great aplomb.

> **TIP:**
> Students and ex-students can be a huge source of positive male role models, not least if among their number we include significant peer leaders. The immense added value is clear, the issuance of an instant licence for any boy to engage in the same activity and emulate the same behaviour.

Application

- Male staff featuring in reading displays, photographed celebrating achievements outside of school – as human beings!
- Male staff talking about their reading in assemblies or about child care, love, peace, environmental issues, animal welfare.
- Male staff heading up charitable causes.
- Male high school staff working in partner primaries – particularly useful if engaged with smashing stereotypes – teaching dance, health and social care issues, singing, textiles.
- Displays of posters of significant caring and heroic males such as Mandela, Gandhi, Geldof.
- Posters from organizations such as the White Ribbon Campaign – men against violence to women (www.whiteribboncampaign.co.uk).
- Significant male students in posters and displays modelling positive learning behaviour.
- Cross-phase work; for example, older boys writing for Nursery (or older, children), projects via email, collaboration in cross-phase drama projects such as Year 10 working with Year 5 on a bullying theme.
- Working as peer befrienders, peer mentors; for example, Year 11 mentoring Year 7.
- High school boys working with Nursery children.
- Peer leaders working on eradicating bullying.
- High school boys at their partner primary schools on work experience.
- High school boys helping with sport and other extra-curricular activities.
- High school boys' work on display (with photographs) in their old primary school.

Concept

Barrier 21 Use of non-performance enhancing drugs

It is no secret that many young men smoke cannabis on a very regular basis, to the great detriment of their health and performance in school. The reasons are many – experimentation, peer pressure, a way of developing confidence and as an aid to relaxation. The search for 'peak' experiences that help them to transcend some of the agonies and unhappy experiences of adolescence are also undoubtedly a huge part of the picture. The dangers of cannabis to the health of young people become greater as more and more potent strains are developed. The most common types now are approximately 40 times stronger than the cannabis smoked during the 1960s. The risks of serious mental health problems occurring in early adulthood are fourfold. Drugs education is clearly not working and many schools simply sweep the issue under the carpet for fear of being labelled a school with a drug problem.

But maybe there is one area that we are yet to explore with any kind of vigour. In *Saving Our Children from Our Chaotic World* (2003), Maggie Dent explores the kinds of alternative experiences of transcendence that we should introduce, explicitly discuss and hopefully engender engagement with as 'alternative highs': 'The Athletic High', the promotion of outdoor pursuits, artistic and musical expression and, perhaps most significantly, 'Nurturing the Inner World'. Should our boys become engaged with the processes of breathing, yoga, meditation, Tai Chi or Chi Kung, then a whole new world can be opened up for them providing them with precisely what it is that they had been seeking in those far more dangerous arenas.

Application

Drug awareness audit

Question	Answer	Action?
Is our drug education programme powerful enough?		
Do our students believe that it is?		
Do we know how extensive the use of cannabis is among our boys?		
Is there anything preventing us from finding out?		
Do we understate the extent of cannabis use?		
Do we have a cannabis problem in school?		
Do we ever directly address users with the issues?		
Do our students ever hear real first-hand experiences of heavy drug users?		
Do our students ever hear real first-hand experiences of people achieving 'natural highs'?		
Do we ever discuss alternative methods of transcendence at all?		

more question: Is your school brave enough to form the country's 'Natural High Club'?

Concept

Barrier 22 Lack of engagement with the life of the school

Good practice abounds in primary schools where boys are massively engaged with the life of their schools, running the office, the ICT suite, the library, even running the headteacher! Perhaps the most exciting example I have come across is Grange School in Derbyshire. On Fridays, the pupils do not go to school they go to 'Grangeton' (it is the same building). They have a council, including a mayor (all trained by their local MP, and as part of their training they spend a day in parliament, and the mayor also acts as a governor of the school). The town has its own newspaper (whose staff are trained by the local newspaper) and a radio station (whose employees are trained by local radio personnel). The TV station runs its own talent shows and the town also includes its own museum and craft centre – trained by the local museum service – a language café, a job centre (where everyone applies for jobs in the first place) and even G-Bay for selling parents' unwanted items!

How often are your boys given anything like this level of responsibility for their own learning? How often have you engaged them in any form of whole-school decision making or share in their perceptions? Here are some other real-life examples:

- 'Big ears' – an innovation in a south London school where school stops ten minutes early on Fridays and pupils sit in groups of six with any adult in school to share their thoughts and feelings on school (corridors are adorned with Photoshopped pictures of staff with big ears).
- Friday parliament – a school in West Yorkshire runs its own full-blown parliament once a week to discuss hot school issues.
- 'Pick six' – one headteacher in the Midlands picks six pupils every week to conduct an in-depth interview relating to some area of current interest in the scho

Application

Running a successful Year 6 boys' conference

Sometimes boys need a little encouragement from outside to take more of an active role in the life of their school. The following is based on four conferences run by the author in Kirklees.

Aims

- To celebrate boys' successes publicly and enthusiastically.
- To enable boys to share a collective experience in creative, expressive and performing arts that says to them 'If you are engaged with the affective side of the curriculum now, we want you to know just how much we value and respect that in our high schools.'
- To enable boys to listen to and work with a number of positive male role models who model a caring masculinity.
- To enable them to learn new skills that will not only aid transition but also improve the quality of their lives at school.
- To send them back to school as ambassadors, feeding back to school councils and assemblies, and instigating projects such as peer befriending, buddying schemes, Investors in Pupils, and effective school council work.

The process

- As a family, cluster, pyramid or even whole local authority of schools, determine how many boys and teachers you can accommodate. Ideal number is 15–20 schools with six pupils and one teacher from each. (I always requested boys who had achieved in a range of ways in school, although the choice is yours!)
- Provide the most luxurious setting (and refreshments) that the budget will allow.
- Invite the local press.
- Provide a small room to operate as a 'Big Brother Diary Room' where boys can drop in during breaks and answer a series of questions about the value of the day, what difference it will make to them, and what they intend to do when they return to school.

(*continued on page 73*)

Concept

The school tour: where would your visitors be led?

Being taken around a school by a couple of Year 11 boys is invariably an education! On one such visit, I asked them to take me to points of interest, telling them I had limited time available. First port of call was the dining room. Idly remarking that it resembled a fast food outlet, replete with photographs of the kind of food you would like to think you were getting, I was quickly put to rights, 'It's not like that at all, sir. In fact, the school council regularly discusses the food that is served and how we can provide a healthy diet.'

The second port of call was the CDT area. The display was staggering. Every square inch of wall on the corridor was filled with coursework. A whole wall was given over to an A* folder of work, and next to it a giant 'A*'. Similarly another wall featured a C folder, with a giant 'C' emblazoned next to it. The boys stood there, eyeing the work, waiting for my next blundering comment.

'So you like this then?' I asked, cagily, 'Why?'

'Well, without it we wouldn't know what an A* really looks like, would we?'

Third stop was the corridor outside the RE department, where happy, smiling pictures of pupils adorned a huge display. Unlike any other pictures of pupils in the building these were on a meaningful, eye-catching scale. Seeing their two grinning faces appearing from the midst of the display, I did not need to ask any more dumb questions. It was obvious that here were two boys who were proud to be part of their school, have their voices heard, their needs met and their successes celebrated.

Application

Running a successful Year 6 boys' conference continued

The process continued

- Provide a huge wall to display work that the boys are encouraged to bring in. Call it 'WONDERWALL!' The work can represent any area of which they are proud – photographs of achievements, certificates, poems and so on. (One workshop could even turn this work into the basis of a website.)
- Plan for three or four 15–20 minute presentations to start the day. A motivational introduction, followed by a selection of the following: a rapper, a street dancer, poet, author, artist, book illustrator, musician, songwriter, music producer, DJ, storyteller, puppeteer.
- Allow a luxurious break time – 'Would you care for a Danish pastry, sir?' can make someone's day!
- After the break, run a series of workshops that might include a selection of the following in addition to workshops run by your writers, artists, dancers and so on: drama/role play, peer tutor training, Befriending skills, controlling and expressing emotions, dealing with peer pressure, developing a website, writing an article on how boys can succeed for the local press.
- Run parallel sessions for accompanying teachers on a range of Raising Boys' Achievement-related issues.
- Have a wonderful lunch! (Encouraging contributions to the diary room and discussing each other's contributions to the Wonderwall.)
- Begin the afternoon with a couple more short, sharp presentations.
- Repeat the workshops for students and separate staff workshops.
- Watch roughly edited (whatever time allows) footage from the diary room.
- Provide everyone with a range of ideas for feedback and mini projects back at school; together with a 'good news' postcard for boys to return with news of their work back at school that is a direct outcome of the day.
- Publish and disseminate outcomes.

Concept

Barrier 23 Parents' lack of understanding of the role they can play

It can often seem to be the case that we spend our days nurturing, encouraging and, hopefully, educating our boys, writing as it were on an internal whiteboard, only to see that every night they go home and the whiteboard is wiped clean. They return the next day, we write on the internal whiteboard, and again the whiteboard is wiped clean. Of course, it is true that in some cases we have parents who are reflecting their own negative experiences of school onto their sons, which makes it hard to develop positive relationships that might move us forward BUT we have to try. The truth is that many parents of boys desperately need our help and guidance.

At a very basic level, there are, as can be seen in these pages, ways of communicating the right kinds of messages regarding:

- the need to encourage boys to talk openly
- the need to consider how we talk to them
- the need to provide positive male role models
- the need to develop independence.

Steve Biddulph, author of numerous books on boys, suggests that parents need to:

- spend time with their boys – there are many parents now who are money rich but time poor.
- play rough and tumble – boys do need physicality.
- teach them respect for women.
- show them what a decent man is.
- honour their tender feelings.
- ensure that they do their fair share of housework!

'We really disable our boys when we do everything for them.'

Application

Running a parents' evening: 'Let's Hear it for the Boys!'

- ■ Lay it on the line with the publicity! I used the following at the first ever boys' parents' evening I ran and I've been using it ever since!

  A lot of boys don't…
    - – do as well in tests as girls do
    - – read as much as girls do
    - – work as neatly as girls do
    - – like doing homework
    - – organize themselves very well
    - – come prepared to lessons
    - – work hard in case they are made fun of
    - – work too hard when they are young but still expect to do well at 16.

  The truth is it shows … What can WE do about it?

- ■ Sounds basic, but make parents comfortable, and let them know it will only last an hour.

- ■ Begin with general points regarding physiological needs. Is he having breakfast? (If not, then by 10.30 am he has the reaction speed of a 70 year old!) Talk about hydration, sleep and so on.

- ■ Talk about the problems we have before we even start – about how boys are demonized in the media, in their neighbourhood. In their home.

- ■ Fill them in with the facts. You might ask for a show of hands of those who believe that boys do better at KS1? 2? 3? In English? Maths? Science? At GCSE in English? Art? PE? Design technology?

- ■ Talk about some of the reasons. You might want to cover language development – stressing the need to talk and encourage and support reading – or peer pressure and the need to be ever vigilant, or teaching and learning styles (doing a learning styles questionnaire together with their boys can be a fascinating experience – not least as it shows parents why their sons never sit at that new desk they bought them!)

- ■ Talk about how they might help – points from the leaflet (see pages 77 and 79) produced by parents at my own school could help!

Concept

Prompt sheet for parents' evening leaflet (1)

1. Boys need lots of praise and encouragement – some would say even more than girls – to keep them on an even keel!

2. Reading is absolutely vital and fiction is particularly important. Boys need to learn to reflect – reading fiction really helps. If he needs help to choose, his teacher, librarian or a good bookseller will help (teachers note the booklist on page 27 for top junior/lower secondary boys). Many need to see males reading because they think it is for girls!

3. Standing on the sidelines of a junior football match as a permanent reserve, in the hail and the snow, will do little for his self-esteem.

4. **The big one!** Remember, if we do everything for our boys, we hugely disable them.

5. Boys are at school for about 15 per cent of their time – there are hundreds of learning opportunities outside school – starting in your front room.

6. Boys are led to believe (by other boys and by their role models and heroes) that expressing emotions is not what boys do and it is vital they do not end up having to choose other means of expressing themselves.

7. It is important that he sees that you are interested to know that he is on top of things – and praise him for it!

8. It is vitally important that he is organizing HIMSELF.

9. Peer pressure or the 'anti-swot' or 'anti-boff' culture is very common among boys and one of the biggest causes of boys' underachievement. It is really important that you are alert to any signs.

Application

Parents' evening leaflet (1)

1. Give lots of encouragement to boost confidence!

2. If your son has a reading habit, encourage it. If not, do your best to help him develop one. You could ask his teacher's advice. Seeing other males around the house reading can also help.

3. Guide him towards out-of-school activities that he will not only enjoy but at which he can also succeed.

4. Give him more responsibilities around the house – **do not** do everything for him.

5. Try to create some opportunities for learning at home by discussing the news or TV programmes.

6. Persuade him that talking over feelings is best, as it helps release tension and anger.

7. Check his student planner regularly (if he has one).

8. Make sure he gets **himself** properly organized in time. 'Planning and preparation help prevent poor performance.'

9. Contact school immediately if you feel your son is under pressure from others not to work.

Concept

Prompt sheet for parents' evening leaflet (2)

10. Schools, particularly primary schools, are very short of adult male role models. Members of your own extended family and family friends could be a vital source of help and support here.

11. Siblings and older relatives can often be a real encouragement and incentive to work – particularly if they are enthusiastic about it! But beware of making comparisons – 'I wish you worked as hard as your sister' is not an incentive for many boys to work harder!

12. You may like to communicate the point that until we have slept, no learning from the previous day has had time to filter through into the brain – the less you sleep, the less you learn. Eight hours has to be an absolute minimum!

13. Research shows that parents (especially mothers) spend more time talking about feelings with their daughters than their sons (except for anger and fear, interestingly!) – and we all know what could happen when feelings are not allowed out.

14. Teachers want happy, confident and motivated students and they want to know how they can work together with parents to make them that way. Make the most of your son's teachers!

15. Short-term rewards really help. Something small at teatime rather than the promise of a huge gift at the end of the year often works best! (Actually they would prefer both!)

16. It is perhaps easier said than done to reduce leisure time spent in front of screens but you need to know – and so does he – that it can have a depressing effect, not to mention the health risks.

17. Organization and routines do not always come naturally – they might need some rules in this area. As for the right environment for learning, we are all different. Maybe he can work with music on and slumped across the bed, in dim light. Ask him!

18. Getting him to talk and reflect on his learning definitely can really help, but again it does not come naturally to many boys. Ask him, 'Did you ask any good questions today?'

Application

Parents' evening leaflet (2)

10.	Good male role models can play a significant part in boys' education; for example, by reading to them, giving help with work at home, or even by helping out at school.
11.	Other learners in the house can be used as good examples.
12.	Make sure he has enough sleep!
13.	Reassure him that it is OK to express his feelings, in fact positively encourage it.
14.	Talk to his teacher whenever you are concerned.
15.	Have your own system of rewards at home for good work and behaviour.
16.	Limit leisure time spent in front of screens.
17.	When he starts to be given homework, get into the habit of making sure that he does it on the night that it is set – preferably as soon as he gets home and definitely without the TV on.
18.	Show interest in his day at school.

Whole school

Concept

Barrier 24 Playtimes for boys tend to be hyperphysical

There are lots of ways in which we can not only change the nature of lunchtimes and playtimes or breaks but also how we can create the right kind of physical and emotional environment for learning. Structured play in primary schools, the provision of rooms for board games, the development of social areas and a range of activities for boys who do not want to be charging around the playground are considered, as is peer massage (from early years up to Year 8) and yoga in school.

> Peer massage makes me feel warm and relaxed.
> It makes me feel appreciated.
>
> Year 6 boys

Activities that take the macho edge out of those energetic masses that enter the classroom after breaks are significant if we want to get the best out of boys in the classroom.

> I wouldn't have believed it possible but Year 11 boys performing basic Indian head massage techniques on each other has been amazingly popular and effective at calming them down. They didn't think twice about it!
>
> Year 11 teacher

TIP:
Consideration of heating and lighting can be most significant too. Boys prefer cooler temperatures and all young people need less light than adults do! Indeed, if you wish to create exactly the right environment for learning ask them the question yourself. How might we best prepare ourselves to learn?

Application

Breathing – 'getting in the flow'

- Settle the group – with eyes open, sitting comfortably, feet flat on the floor, spine naturally upright and shoulders open, imagining a golden thread pulling their heads straight.

- Ask them to breathe in to the count of four – a deep full breath, engaging the abdomen. Hold for four. Release for four. Repeat the process twice more. Ask them to imagine they are breathing in a cool blue and breathing out a misty grey.

- Ask them to notice what sounds they can hear beyond the building. Prompt them if necessary – referring to traffic, voices outside, birdsong and so on. Point out that in this exercise this is not to be a distraction but merely part of the background as they travel deeper inside themselves.

- Ask them to now bring their awareness inside the building, noticing what sounds they can hear as they come closer.

- Then direct them to slowly move their focus to sounds immediately outside the room > inside the room > then closer, to their own breathing > to the tips of their noses and then, ultimately, to the sounds within. Invite them to listen to their own internal chatter. Anything that is bothering them put in an imaginary 'botheration box' and set aside.

- Fix their attention on their own breathing. Does it feel cool? Warm? Are the breaths rapid or calm? Get them to notice what is happening physically to the chest. (When breathing in, the whole class will slow down, it is called entrainment – a similar effect to a room full of clocks when all the pendulums move in sync.)

- Using the colour blue, students need to think of cool streams, sparkling rivers, tranquil seas. Prompt with, 'Use the calmness of the waters you can see and hear to relax the body, washing over, running through, taking with it any tensions and stress, cares and worries. Leaving you feeling calm, cleansed, refreshed, alert, focused and recharged.'

- Now bring them back allowing the picture of the river to fade and reversing the stages of awareness back to the body.

Concept

Barrier 25 Homophobic bullying

Homophobic bullying is widely used by boys in particular as a way of policing what is acceptable and what is unacceptable male behaviour, and as such can affect more than non-heterosexual boys. Whenever or wherever it is felt to be fashionable to use the term 'gay', it is often used to describe the kind of things that **real** boys don't do, such as work hard or care about things or have feelings, 'I'm not going to do my do my homework – it's gay.' In this context alone, it is hugely unhelpful as it represents another very powerful weapon in the Peer Police's armoury. When used against youngsters who *are* gay, the damage, as can be seen in the invaluable National Healthy School Standard publication *Stand Up For Us* (HDA nd), can be devastating.

Pupils who are victims of homophobic bullying:
- have higher levels of absenteeism and truancy;
- are less likely to enter higher or further education;
- are more likely to contemplate self-harm and suicide.

More than 40 per cent of lesbian, gay and bisexual men and women who had been bullied at school made at least one attempt to self-harm, while more than 20 per cent had attempted suicide (Rivers 2001; Mullen 1999). A recent DfES survey revealed that only 6 per cent of school bullying policies specifically referred to homophobic bullying. Perhaps this is the most disturbing fact of all. For the sake of these young people, schools need to ensure that it is widely understood that:
- homophobic language and abuse is unacceptable;
- incidents will be consistently and firmly dealt with;
- such incidents will be recorded whether perpetrators are pupils or adults;
- perpetrators and victims will receive appropriate support and guidance;
- adults may face disciplinary procedures.

Application

For discussion

Homophobic bullying incident log. Two teachers in one school collected these examples in three weeks. What do you think?

Date	Type of incident – verbal or physical abuse (please record words said)	Perpetrator and target/person being bullied
21/1	Boy X's bag stolen by group of boys in his class, all books vandalized, graffitied – 'X is a gay bastard'.	Four Year 8 boys and fellow Year 8
21/1	'They are gay' – verbal reference to the RAF.	Year 11 boy
23/1	Refusal to sit next to pupil Y – 'He smells, he's gay.'	Two Year 10 boys of another
26/1	'Look at A's trainers, they're so gay!'	Year 9 girl to fellow Year 9 about classmate
28/1	'Battyman'	Year 8 to fellow Year 8
3/2	'What's this boys? – A mothers' meeting?'	Staff member to seven boys in Year 10
8/2	'He looks like a girl' – verbal abuse.	Two Year 10 boys
9/2	'Don't be such a sissy.'	Staff member to Year 9 boy
14/2	'Bender' 'Gay' – verbal abuse directed at goalkeeper having conceded another goal.	Year 10 and 11 spectating at football game
18/2	'You're a f...ing bender.'	Year 11 boy to another
18/2	'Your mum's a lez, I've seen her snogging her girlfriend.'	Year 9 girl to another
20/2	'Fairy'	Teacher to Year 8 boy
21/2	'She's a geezer bird.'	Year 10 comment about a Year 12 girl
21/2	'Come on then girls' – said to a group of boys.	Staff member to Year 7 boys
22/2	'You're so gay.'	Year 10 girl to Year 10 boy
22/2	'That ain't natural man!' and 'Stab him up, he's a battyman!'	Reference to Boy George by Year 11 boys

(Source: *Stand Up For Us* (HDA nd) adapted from 'Tackling homophobic bullying in schools', Bolton Homophobic Forum June 2001)

Barrier 26 Inappropriate reward systems

By and large, boys love rewards. In fact, it is often argued that boys need a disproportionate amount in order to keep them happy. Certainly many boys prefer short-term rewards and short-term gratification. Yet it is not uncommon for boys to shy away from receiving rewards publicly. The celebratory arena is a very popular patrol ground for the Peer Police. As we know, peer pressure prevents so many boys not only from celebrating achievements but also from striving to achieve in case a reward is forthcoming.

So how would it be if:

- boys were encouraged to have diaries containing secret dreams of success with space to note down every positive comment that anyone makes about their progress towards those dreams.
- we set 'praise targets' for staff and pupils, so that everyone was given the challenge to praise three people every day for what they have done, how they look or because of the kind of person they are!
- we sent beautiful praise postcards home that the biggest reprobate in school will have displayed on his fridge until the day he retires.
- we made classrooms 'build up' zones instead of 'put down' zones.
- teachers congratulated each other regularly in public and regularly celebrated their own success.
- we were to 'Go large' with celebrations thus normalizing the process and removing stigma.

Cautionary tale: watching a group of boys in a classroom the other day, I heard a teacher enthusiastically greet a boy's cursory response to a question thus, 'Michael, that was a stunning response!' It was not and Michael knew it was not. He did not answer any more questions. It is, above all, the genuine interest of another human being that boys often crave and we must supply them with the environment in which they can genuinely celebrate it.

Application

Rewards system

Your perceptions:

- Do boys continue to feel comfortable about accepting rewards all the way through your school?
- If it begins to lose currency at a certain point, do you understand the reasons why?
- Are staff consistent in handing out rewards, and do students notice?
- Are boys and girls equally represented in public celebrations of success?
- Was your current reward system more effective two years ago?
- In your view, is the reward system you employ generally working for boys?
- What steps can be taken to improve it? (Answer: Well you could begin by asking them! Use the following as a basis for a survey of student opinion.)

Students' perceptions: Is it cool...?

- When a teacher writes a good comment on your work?
- When your work is put on display?
- When a teacher comments about your work in front of the rest of the class?
- When you get a merit or a credit?
- When the teacher asks you to read out your work?
- Receiving an award in assembly?
- When you are asked to demonstrate or talk about something you know to others?
- When you get a letter or a postcard home saying that you have done well?

Barrier 27 Intervention occurring too late

It was often the tradition to take a group of boys on one side, usually the 'boys on the borderline', and tell them 'come on lads you can do it!' Last-minute mentoring. Far too little, too late. This is not to say that there is no place for this, provided it meets the boys' criteria. According to the Homerton report (Younger and Warrington, 2005), boys like mentors who have patience, who listen and who are enthusiastic for them yet accept their faults. They need mentors who are straight talking, honest, genuine and who not only provide advice, support and strategies but also ensure that they place responsibility firmly back with them, not just do everything for them.

Thinking earlier, group mentoring in Year 8 can provide a very positive service at a critical time for many boys. I have worked with such groups, focusing on raising motivation scores and aspirations – handled well a 'Hidden Talent Group' can easily be steered away from stigma. But interventions are frequently required far earlier. What is happening in terms of peer pressure at the point of transition when all those diverse cultures clash and boys jockey for position? How can you identify and ameliorate the negative impact? What is happening in terms of developing self-esteem levels as boys progress through primary school? Are we monitoring and seeking to address these issues as well as giving support for problems with developing literacy skills? Earlier still, how carefully are we monitoring and seeking to address emotional intelligence issues such as impulse control, empathy and, perhaps most importantly of all, boys' developing abilities as reflective human beings? Are we considering in what ways we might engage parents' support from pre-school right through to GCSE, guiding them in ways to support their boys?

There are many vital ways and times at which we need to plan intervention beyond responding to scores and levels and for far more honourable reasons than massaging examination results.

Application

Intervention – the rough guide

Consider what measures you might use to monitor the following.

What strategies might be used to make a positive impact in these areas?

Developing independence skills

Early signs of gender-stereotypical behaviour

Developing impulse control

Physical problems with early writing

Developing self-esteem levels

Developing skills of reflection

Early signs of peer pressure

Identity issues at transition

Motivational levels at Year 8

Laddish behaviour

Organizational skills

Levels of aspiration in Year 9

Depth of impact of peer pressure in Years 10 and 11

Concept

Barrier 28 Teachers' lack of awareness of the barriers to boys' learning

BUT NOT YOU if you have read this or *Breaking through Barriers to Boys' Achievement* or both!

You may wish to complete the plenary maps on the facing page to remind yourself of the complexity of the issue.

EVEN BETTER – ask the real experts. Ask the boys themselves. Using the same simple map, and without any reading or discussion, set up the following process and see what you get!

The process

1. Divide the boys into groups of six, giving them time to allocate themselves roles.

    Writer   You write down the main points that the group come up with.

    Encourager In a very friendly way, you make sure that everyone feels part of the work and everyone takes part.

    Timer   You keep an eye on how the group is getting on and gently speed them up if anyone is wasting time.

    Speaker   You will be asked to tell the rest of the class at the end what your group found out.

    Manager   You are in charge, but you must not do it in a bossy way. You start things off and then ask others to take their turn.

    Director   You make sure that people do not start going off the subject. Gently bring them back to the task by asking questions.

2. Give them precisely two minutes to add their thoughts to the central idea, in the form of a simple map.
3. STOP and pass on the map to another group. Repeat the process.
4. Repeat the process one more time.
5. Do the second map!

Application

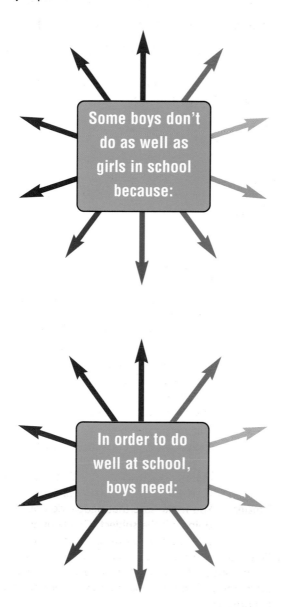

Some boys don't do as well as girls in school because:

In order to do well at school, boys need:

Concept

I believe that not only are boys the real experts, knowing exactly what the issues are *and* how they might be solved, I also believe that one of the most effective strategies is to show them that *you are on their case!*

One group of Year 10 boys in a high school recently informed me that boys do not do as well as girls in school because:

- they were easily distracted;
- they played around a lot more;
- some teachers concentrated more on giving them 'comments' than teaching them;
- they had shorter concentration spans;
- teachers preferred girls;
- girls were more organized.

They told me that they like teachers who:

- are down to earth;
- talk about the outside world;
- are funny;
- let you talk so long as you do not go too far;
- do not have you writing all the time;
- respect you.

But they did not like teachers who:

- patronize you;
- are sarcastic;
- are argumentative;
- tell you you have a fresh start but do not really mean it;
- just 'babble on' all the time;
- make you copy things out all the time.

And that they could improve if they:

- had more belief in themselves;
- forgot about their mates in lesson time;
- got organized;
- listened more;
- made a few sacrifices now for the sake of their future;
- someone made them feel that they could amount to something.

Application

Sharing expertise between staff

- 'Speed dating' – a carousel of presentations of successful classroom strategies and approaches presented by the teachers concerned in their own classrooms (Sydney Stringer School).
- Family, cluster or pyramid of schools newsletter highlighting good practice, working group minutes, reports on courses attended and relevant resources (Gender and Achievement Working Party – 'GAWP': Newsome 'pyramid' early 1990s).
- Staffroom Raising Boys' Achievement project boards (Colne Valley High School).
- Staffroom washing line – to peg new ideas and innovations to.
- Thursday morning hotspot – staff are allowed five minutes at a staff briefing to talk about a new, successful initiative.
- 'Tig' observation – started by the head of a project team or department, any member of staff can drop in to observe a lesson that involves a new strategy. Then it is the turn of the person who has been observed to 'tig' someone else by visiting them. A 'tig' file is kept of all good practice seen (Norham Community Technical College).
- Whole authority newsletter, sharing good practice, innovations, course information, boys' work, resources (Kirklees).
- Cross-phase conferences (that may develop into cross-phase working groups) to share successful innovations and encourage continuity.

It is sad isn't it, that while sharing good practice in medicine is part and parcel of everyday life, in education we often feel we don't want to 'show off'. Let's get over it! Those Peer Police get everywhere don't they!

Barrier to boys' learning: checklist	Strategy
1. Lack of independence prior to starting school Evidence:	
2. Less developed linguistically on entry to school Evidence:	
3. Made to read and write before being physically or emotionally ready Evidence:	
4. Many writing activities seen as irrelevant and unimportant Evidence:	
5. Difficulties with structuring written work Evidence:	
6. Reticent to spend time on planning and preparation Evidence:	
7. Reading fiction perceived as a female province Evidence:	

Barrier to boys' learning: checklist	Strategy
8. Mismatch of teaching and learning styles Evidence:	
9. Lack of opportunities for reflection Evidence:	
10. Inappropriate pupil grouping Evidence:	
11. Inappropriate seating arrangements Evidence:	
12. Ineffective group-work Evidence:	
13. Mismatch in assessment and boys' preferred ways of working Evidence:	
14. Emotional intelligence issues Evidence:	

Barrier to boys' learning: checklist	Strategy
15. Low self-esteem and limiting self-beliefs Evidence:	
16. Teacher talk/Teachers' expectations Evidence:	
17. Peer pressure (anti-swot culture) Evidence:	
18. Laddish culture Evidence:	
19. The influence of street culture Evidence:	
20. The lack of positive male role models Evidence:	
21. The use of non-performance enhancing drugs Evidence:	

Barrier to boys' learning: checklist	Strategy
22. Lack of engagement with the life of the school Evidence:	
23. Parents' lack of understanding of the role they can play Evidence:	
24. Playtimes for boys tend to be hyperphysical Evidence:	
25. Homophobic bullying Evidence:	
26. Inappropriate reward systems and the lack of a positive achievement culture Evidence:	
27. Intervention occurring too late Evidence:	
28. Teachers' lack of awareness of the barriers to boys' learning Evidence:	

Which three priority areas will you address first?

1. _____

2. _____

3. _____

Further reading

Armitage, S. (1993), *Book of Matches*, Faber and Faber, London

Askew, M. and Wiliam, D. (1995), *Recent Research in Mathematics Education 5–16*, HMSO, London

Ball, K. and Wilson, G. (2004), *Don' Stagn8 Innov8*, Kirklees School Effectiveness Service

Biddulph, S. (1998), *Raising Boys*, Thorsons, London

Canfield, J. (2000), *Chicken Soup for the Soul*, Vermillion, London

Dennison, P. (1989), *Brain Gym*, Edu-Kinesthetics, Inc., Ventura, Ca.

Dent, M. (2003), *Saving Our Children from Our Chaotic World*, Pennington Publications, Australia

Ginnis, P. (2001), *Teacher's Toolkit*, Crown House, Bancyfelin

Ginott, H.G. (1972), *Teacher and Child*, MacMillan, Basingstoke

Health Development Agency (no date) *Stand Up For Us: Challenging Homophobia in Schools*, NHSS and DfES. Downloadable from www.wiredforhealth.gov.uk

Kindlon, D. and Thompson, M. (1999), *Raising Cain: Protecting the Emotional Life of Boys*, Ballantine Books, New York

Lucas, B. and Smith, A. (2002), *How to Help Your Child Succeed*, Network Educational Press, Stafford

Mullen, A. (1999), *Social Inclusion, Reaching Out to Bisexual, Gay and Lesbian Youth*, ReachOUT, Reading

Rivers, I. (2001), 'The bullying of sexual minorities at school', *Educational and Child Psychology*, vol. 18 (1), 33–46

Smith, A. (2002), *Move It*, Network Educational Press, Stafford

Wilson, G. (1990), *Roots and Routes*, Nelson, Cheltenham (out of print)

Wilson, G. (2002), *Let's Hear it for the Boys* (parents' leaflet), Kirklees LEA

Wilson, G. (2003), *Using the National Healthy School Standard to Raise Boys' Achievement*, NHSS and DfES

Wilson, G. (2006), *Breaking through Barriers to Boys' Achievement*, Network Continuum Education, London

Younger, M. and Warrington, M. (2005), *Raising Boys' Achievement*, Final report (Homerton College, Cambridge), DfES, Nottingham